OPERATION
MINDFUCK

Also by Robert Guffey

OPERATION MINDFUCK

QAnon and the Cult of Donald Trump

ROBERT GUFFEY

OR Books
New York · London

To Joan d'Arc

(HunterGatheress, Fortean Journalist &
Fabulist Fiction Writer),

who published my first article 25 years ago

CONTENTS

"In regard to propaganda the early advocates of universal literacy and a free press envisaged only two possibilities: the propaganda might be true, or it might be false. They did not foresee what in fact has happened, above all in our Western capitalist democracies—the development of a vast mass communications industry, concerned in the main neither with the true nor the false, but with the unreal, the more or less totally irrelevant. In a word, they failed to take into account man's almost infinite appetite for distractions."

—Aldous Huxley, *Brave New World Revisited*, 1958

INTRODUCTION

ZERO HOUR, 2021

and other epic stupidities
of the 21st century

"People ask me to predict the Future, when all I want to do is prevent it."

—Ray Bradbury, *Yestermorrow*, 1991

Ray Bradbury published his short story "Zero Hour" in the Fall 1947 issue of the science fiction magazine, *Planet Stories*. Most readers will have discovered the tale in Bradbury's 1951 collection, *The Illustrated Man*. Over the decades, it's been adapted to radio, comic books, television, and film. The main character of the story is Mary Morris, the mother of a seven-year-old girl named Mink who's obsessed with a trendy new children's game called "Invasion." Mink tells her mother that she has a new friend named Drill who can travel to other "dimens-shuns," but Drill needs "kids under nine" (who are impressionable and free of skepticism) to be able to see and understand him and ultimately pull him and his people into our plane of existence. Only at that moment, referred to by Mink as "zero hour," can the invasion begin. At lunchtime, Mink explains the origins of the game to her mother:

> "They couldn't figure a way to attack, Mom. Drill says—he
> says in order to make a good fight you got to have a new way

of surprising people. That way you win. And he says also you got to have help from your enemy."

"A fifth column," said Mom.

"Yeah. That's what Drill said. And they couldn't figure a way to surprise Earth or get help."

"No wonder. We're pretty darn strong." Mom laughed, cleaning up. Mink sat there, staring at the table, seeing what she was talking about.

"Until, one day," whispered Mink melodramatically, "they thought of children!"

Of course, Mary thinks her daughter is making all of this up out of her own seven-year-old imagination. Later that day, however, Mary happens to be talking on the phone with her old friend, Helen. Helen lives in Scranton, Pennsylvania and Mary lives in New York. Helen mentions, in passing, that her son Tim's "got a crush on some guy named—*Drill*, I think it was." Mary assumes "Drill" must be a new "password" and expresses astonishment that this "Invasion" game has already spread to another state. Helen goes on to say that their mutual friend, Josephine, who lives in Boston, mentioned to her earlier that her own kids had begun playing the "Invasion" game recently. "It's sweeping the country," Helen says.

Neither of the women can figure out how this odd new game, with the same unfathomable "passwords" and rules, could have spread among so many disconnected children so quickly. Needless to say, even in this futuristic tale (which appears to be set a generation after World War II, based on Mary's comment to Helen, "Were we this bad when we were kids in '48?"), the internet has not yet been invented. So how do trends spread among the immature and the vulnerable in a pre-8chan society? Mary doesn't know the answer to that question, of course, but it's the peculiar similarities of the "Invasion" stories that first tip Mary to the notion that this "game" isn't imaginary at all. Perhaps the whole enterprise started off as nothing more than a lark for the gullible Mink, but it's now become very real and is threatening the security of the entire adult world.

★

Articles that attempted to deal with the QAnon phenomenon on a somewhat serious level began popping up more and more during the first few months of 2020, right around the time the dark reality of the COVID-19 pandemic began to descend on the public at large. The mainstream response to QAnon, even following the insurrection, tends to range from the dismissive to the naïve, and proposed strategies for dealing with the spread of QAnon-inspired disinformation range from the nonexistent to the underwhelming. On February 18, 2021, *The Atlantic* published an article by Barbara Fister entitled "The Librarian War Against QAnon":

> . . . QAnon is something of a syncretic religion. But its influence doesn't stop with religious communities. While at its core it's a 21st-century reboot of a medieval anti-Semitic trope (blood libel), it has shed some of its Christian vestments to gain significant traction among non-evangelical audiences.[1]

Despite being perceptive enough to identify the medieval origins of QAnon's fanatical obsession with the notion that innocent children are being kidnapped from their bedrooms and harvested by the "elites," Fister concludes her piece by saying that that the best way to combat QAnon is to change "how education approaches information-literacy instruction." After the destructive events of January 6, 2021, Fister's wide-eyed approach to the problem seems both charming and dangerous. It was partly this dangerous naivety among entrenched political commentators that convinced me to begin writing about QAnon from a perspective slightly different from what I was seeing in mainstream publications during the first few months of 2020.

After the COVID-19 lockdown, it seemed to me that a lot of journalists must have begun reaching out to friends and family with whom they hadn't communicated in quite a long time. A national emergency will do that, I suppose. Over the course of these conversations, strange pronouncements and predictions no doubt began spilling from the mouths of these acquaintances and siblings and parents, etc. Soon afterwards, the journalists started talking to each other and comparing notes. As they tried to puzzle through bizarre passwords, codenames and games they'd never heard of before, their bemused conversations might have been somewhat similar to the one Mary and Helen have in "Zero Hour."

"Black hats."

"White hats."

"Deep Underground Military Bases."

"Save the children."

"Where we go one we go all."

"The storm is coming."

"The Great Awakening is approaching."

"Trust the plan."

"Dark to light."

"Future proves past."

"The military is the only way."

"We are the news."

"There's Q and there's anons."

I don't care if you identify with the left or the right or some
nebulous political party that exists somewhere in between, if
you meet someone who begins spouting—without irony or
humor—unimaginative, pre-scripted slogans you've seen posted
a thousand times on the internet, run in the opposite direction as
fast as you can. There lies the Village of the Damned.

I watched with increasing bemusement as these professional
journalists attempted to wrap their heads around the QAnon
phenomenon while it spread like a communicable disease across
the United States and beyond.

"So have you ever heard of a character named 'Drill'?"
"What about this weird game 'Invasion'? What the hell's all that
nonsense about anyway?"

I quickly came to the conclusion that these reporters weren't
equipped to handle the story in a comprehensive way. Though
they could report reliably on certain isolated aspects of the phenomenon, they seemed incapable of perceiving the Big Picture.
Nothing in their personal experience had prepared them for
this contingency. They might be qualified for other stories of
national interest, but not this one.

I wished somebody with the wherewithal and the necessary
amount of patience would deconstruct the increasingly insane
QAnon phenomenon by tracing all the obscure roots of its convoluted mythos in a simple, straightforward manner that a casual
reader could understand easily, and in this way unveil the con-
siderable unacknowledged debt the QAnon architects owed to a
mélange of pop culture artifacts, early twentieth-century pulp
literature, 1990s DIY conspiracy zines, and paranoid propaganda
well over a hundred years old.

Since I didn't see anyone else attempting this brain-numbing task, I decided, What the hell? Why don't I step in and take a shot at it?

After all, who else would be stupid enough to attempt such a thing?

★

These days, the inability to deal with reality as it exists—and not as one wishes it to exist—is the biggest challenge facing both the right *and* the left. The reaction to QAnon, pre-insurrection, is the perfect example of this trend toward puritanical solipsism. The attitude seems to be: If we block out (or "deplatform") people with whom we disagree, then the Evil Nasty Ones will magically—*poof!*—disappear simply because we can't see or hear them anymore. Like tossing a bucket of water on the Wicked Witch of the West or running a lightsaber through some cloaked asshole at the end of a *Star Wars* film.

I hate to break it to you, kids, but that's not the way the real world works. Perhaps it was inevitable that generations of children raised on pulp-fiction-inspired fantasies in which the forces of Good inevitably conquer the forces of Evil by the end of Act Four should be so ill-equipped to deal with the messy chaos of vanquishing miscreants and scoundrels in the real world. Light overwhelms Darkness. Darkness can never be vanquished with more Darkness. Authoritarianism cannot be counteracted with more authoritarianism.

It was this kind of hermetically sealed, self-imposed ignorance that caused a lot of otherwise rational people to be caught unawares on January 6, 2021, the day the QAnon-influenced Capitol insurrection damn near turned the whole nation upside down.

All throughout 2020, Q regularly linked to mainstream articles about QAnon and incessantly posted comments that went something like this (I'm paraphrasing, of course), "See? *You're the news now!* These liberal loons wouldn't be talking about any of this if there wasn't some *truth* to this information!" He/she/they particularly enjoyed linking to articles that got major parts of the QAnon story wrong. Q no doubt understood that most professional journalists were not equipped to process this story and loved profiting off certain reporters' attempts to combat the phenomenon with ineffective logic.

It's worth mentioning that Q never once linked to the articles I wrote for *Salon* and *The Evergreen Review* that were the raw material for this book. Why were they among the very few reports that somehow escaped his/her/their attention? Was it because the central thesis of my articles revealed far too much about the true origins—and purposes—of the fantastical QAnon narrative?

The truth should be clear by now. From its very beginning, QAnon was intended to be Trump's Plan B (Plan Q?). If it looked like Trump would lose the 2020 election, this goofy-cum-deadly *Plan 9 from Outer Space* version of a coup d'état was to be activated, the seeds of which had been planted as early as October of 2017 when Q first began dumping "information" on 4chan.

On September 23, 2021, Adam Serwer of *The Atlantic* published an article that laid out the many ways Trump tried to illegally overturn the results of the election:

> Last year, John Eastman, whom CNN describes as an attorney working with Donald Trump's legal team, wrote a preposterous memo outlining how then–Vice President Mike Pence could overturn the 2020 election by fiat or, failing that, throw the election to the House of Representatives, where

Republicans could install Trump in office despite his loss to Joe Biden [. . .]. Prior to November, the possibility of Trump attempting a coup was seen as the deranged fever dream of crazed liberals. But as it turns out, Trump and his advisers had devised explicit plans for reversing Trump's loss. Republican leaders deliberately stoked election conspiracy theories they knew to be false, in order to lay a political pretext for invalidating the results. Now, more than ten months after the election, the country knows of at least five ways in which Trump attempted to retain power despite his defeat.

Serwer then goes on to lay out, in detail, those five methods: "1) Trump tried to pressure secretaries of state to not certify, 2) Trump tried to pressure state legislatures to overturn the results, 3) Trump tried to get the courts to overturn the results, 4) Trump tried to pressure Mike Pence to overturn the results, and 5) when all else failed, Trump tried to get a mob to overturn the results."

Serwer then proceeds to ask an essential question:

Imagine if Pence *had* gone along with Eastman's absurd plan, and a mob had been present at the Capitol to help enforce the decision and menace lawmakers who tried to oppose it— then what? As it stands, the mob ransacked the Capitol and forced lawmakers to flee. Had the mob succeeded at reaching any actual legislators, the consequences could have been catastrophic [. . .].[2]

The failure of the Bay of Pigs invasion in 1961 didn't prevent the Central Intelligence Agency from attempting numerous other illegal, wrongheaded coups in democratically elected countries throughout the latter half of the twentieth century, so I don't see why this Digital Age version of the Bay of Pigs should be any more of a deterrent to the "Christian Patriot" authoritarians who haunt the corridors of power in Washington, D.C.

Meanwhile, potential allies in the cause of combating fascism fritter away their valuable time playing internet sleuths, pouring over endless videos shot on the day of the insurrection, trying to find those telltale clues that will transform the Grotesquely Obvious into a matter of Eternal Debate & Deep Intrigue.

★

In the November 2014 issue of *Fortean Times,* I published an article entitled "Attack of the Poisonous Mushroom Growth!" in which I analyzed how the absurd moral panic sparked by American horror comic books was exploited strategically by right-wing politicians of the 1940s and 1950s to distract the attention of John Q. Citizen far away from a slew of unconstitutional acts being perpetrated by those same politicians. This tidal wave of moral panic emerged from a genuine desire to "save the children." A similar strategy is at work today.

Ardent Q-heads insist that one of their main goals is liberating children from abuse, despite the fact that I could not find a single documented instance of a QAnon follower rescuing a child from the clutches of sexual predators. Indeed, the exact opposite has happened. In her October 15, 2020 *FiveThirtyEight* article entitled "Trump Said QAnon 'Fights' Pedophilia. But The Group Has Made It Harder To Protect Kids," journalist Kaleigh Rogers reports:

> Over the summer, Q followers began using #savethechildren
> to spread [their] conspiracy theory, and it worked. From Aug.
> 9 through Aug. 15, more than 12,000 public Facebook posts
> used the hashtag, according to the social media tracking tool

CrowdTangle. The rest of the year, the hashtag tended to garner fewer than 200 posts per week.

But most of the content shared using #savethechildren was based on a Q-fueled and completely warped picture of what child trafficking looks like in this country. And that has made life difficult for the people who actually do anti-trafficking work.

"It's extraordinarily frustrating," said Lisa Goldblatt Grace, co-founder and executive director of My Life My Choice, an anti-trafficking nonprofit. "We've worked so hard for the last 18 years to shift the narrative and have people understand this is happening in our communities. QAnon instead gives folks this incredibly sensationalized 'other' to fear and be angry about."

In reality, child trafficking in the U.S. doesn't look like a bunch of Hollywood and D.C. elites performing satanic rituals on children they stole from suburban playgrounds. Instead, kids who are sexually exploited are often poor, children of color, immigrants, or some combination of the three, and they've often been in the child welfare system or run away from home. In 2018, 1 in 7 kids who were reported as runaways to the National Center for Missing and Exploited Children were likely victims of child sex trafficking, according to UNICEF [. . .].[3]

Of course, if they wanted to "save the children," Q-heads would be better off volunteering at a homeless shelter or fighting against the draconian anti-choice legislation in Texas that prevents underage females from receiving abortions after having been raped. Or they could just log off the internet and take care of their own children for a change. But that's not quite as exciting as hunting witches. Team QAnon knew all of this well before they began posting on 4chan.

As young Mink says in Bradbury's story, "And they couldn't figure a way to surprise Earth or get help [. . .]. Until, one day, they thought of children!"

Ever since the dawn of the Christian Era, children have made a convenient rallying cry for the sanctimonious and the frustrated and the repressed, and it seems that nothing much has changed in the twenty-first century. Perhaps we all better learn a new lesson or two before "Zero Hour" comes creeping up on us again. Next time, Drill and his friends might actually succeed in winning their crazy little kid's game.

ROBERT GUFFEY
March 2022

PART ONE

DONALD TRUMP SAVED ME FROM BEING EATEN BY UNDERGROUND DEMONS!

(or)

QANONSENSE: THE ULTIMATE CATFISH SCHEME

1. White Hats/Black Hats

I've been involved in the wild world of conspiracy theories for twenty-five years now, ever since I published my first article in the pages of *Paranoia Magazine* in the spring of 1996 when I was twenty-four years old. What most impressed me about *Paranoia* was the anarchy of information available within its pages. It wasn't a right-wing conspiracy magazine. It wasn't a left-wing conspiracy magazine. It didn't even exist *between* these two poles. Its editorial mission (or non-mission) was beholden to values (or non-values) that lay far beyond these limiting parameters, a dedication to cataloging and analyzing the extremes of fringe beliefs from multiple angles. Marshall McLuhan once said, "A point of view can be a dangerous luxury when substituted for insight and understanding."[4] The editors of *Paranoia* dedicated themselves to *not* having a point of view. It was the exact opposite of propaganda. By its very nature, propaganda excludes any information that contradicts or undermines the message the dedicated propagandist is intent on disseminating.

Conspiracy theories have always been used by what we now call "persuasion engineers" as tools of mass indoctrination. A good conspiracy theory that seems plausible and frightening enough can be worth more than a thousand well-reasoned stump speeches.

In my first book, *Cryptoscatology: Conspiracy Theory as Art Form*, I broke conspiracy theories down into five distinct categories: 1) Insanity, 2) Disinformation, 3) Misinformation, 4) Satire, and 5) Legitimate Research. Some theories manage to merge two or more categories into one. Only on very rare occasions do such theories manage to combine *all* five categories. The most recent—and arguably most impactful—strain of this hybrid form of conspiracy-mongering first emerged in 2017, promulgated by an anonymous 4chan poster known only as "Q"—or "QAnon." You heard a lot about this in the run up to the 2020 presidential election, and you'll be hearing about it even more in the near future. At least two QAnon supporters (Marjorie Taylor Greene of Georgia and Lauren Boebert of Colorado) were elected to Congress in November of 2020, and devotees of this particular conspiracy theory eagerly supported the re-election of Donald Trump.

The average person, who has *not* spent the past couple of decades studying the origins of conspiracy theories (a reasonable choice, I might add), would probably not recognize the origins of most of the quasi-surreal elements that make up the convoluted QAnon narrative.

In March of 2020, I was talking to a friend about COVID-19 and the national lockdown. He's ten years older than me and lives in a small town in the Midwest. I live in Long Beach, California. While chatting with him on the phone about all the unexpected difficulties that have arisen from teaching my English classes online, he suddenly volunteered the opinion that COVID-19 would end up being a *positive* development in 2020.

"Yeah?" I asked. "How so?"

He proceeded to tell me, with complete sincerity, that after Trump was re-elected in 2020, he would deliver "free energy" to the people of America. Not only that, he was also going to abolish the income tax. *At that very moment,* United States troops had been deployed underground where they were busy "cleaning out" covert subterranean tunnels, "saving hundreds of children from satanic slaves," and kicking out the "black hats."

Without skipping a beat, my friend then insisted that news of this game-changing development would be "coming out" soon.

"It's a great thing," he told me in measured tones. "Trump will have to use the Emergency Broadcast System to give this news to the American people because the media keeps lying and social media like Twitter and YouTube are censoring and deleting videos that report reality the way it actually is."

Furthermore, my friend said in tones of absolute certainty, Trump supporters working behind the scenes (referred to by my friend as the "white hats") had recently wrested control of the entire Google corporation from devil worshippers, which is why you could now retrieve "accurate information" from that particular search engine.

"Uh . . . where are you getting all this?" I asked.

He seemed reluctant to tell me. At first he hemmed and hawed, then muttered, "Oh . . . just these message boards."

"Well, what message boards?" He wouldn't say. "Could you send me the links?" I asked.

"There *are* no links," he replied.

"No links? What is this, the dark web or something?"

He chuckled. "Kind of."

When I pushed further and asked for more details about this "accurate information," in an urgent whisper he told me to search the word "Adrenochrome" on Google.

★

I first read Hunter S. Thompson's classic nonfiction book, *Fear and Loathing in Las Vegas*, when I was eighteen. I've taught the book in my English Composition classes at Cal State Long Beach, off and on, since 2002. I'm well aware that Thompson's alter ego, Raoul Duke, encounters Adrenochrome when Dr.

Gonzo (Duke's speed-fueled attorney) suggests that he ingest the drug because it "makes pure mescaline seem like ginger beer." He also warns Duke, "You'll go completely crazy if you take too much."[5] Duke claims that the hallucinogenic effects of Adrenochrome work best when the substance is harvested from the adrenaline glands of living human bodies.

Even at the tender age of eighteen, I knew that this inspired idea was one of Thompson's many phantasmagorical asides in an otherwise journalistic narrative. Thompson was famous for these detours into Munchausen-level jabberwocky, like the time he claimed that Sen. Ed Muskie was taking "massive doses" of a psychedelic drug called Ibogaine during the 1972 presidential campaign, a hilarious (and entirely false) tale related in Thompson's *Fear and Loathing on the Campaign Trail.*

On the commentary track that accompanies the 2003 Criterion DVD release of Terry Gilliam's film adaptation of *Fear and Loathing in Las Vegas*, Gilliam confirms that Adrenochrome is "a totally invented nonsense-drug that Hunter [made up]." Gilliam follows this with an eerily prescient statement that almost foreshadows the introduction of the drug into QAnon's ever-expanding mythology: "This scene had such an effect on so many people that afterwards I was hearing kids say, 'Oh, I've had Adrenochrome!' They were talking about where they get it. 'Oh, there's a guy who can get me Adrenochrome.' I just love how the Big Lie always works. It worked for Hitler, and it can work for people like us [i.e., artists and storytellers]."[6]

It appears to be working for QAnon as well, since "totally invented nonsense" has a way of becoming facts in the minds of the gullible, the semi-informed, the frustrated, and the insane.

So I did exactly as my friend suggested. I googled the word "Adrenochrome." Keep in mind that my friend insisted that Trump-supporting "white hats" had taken control of Google, correct? Therefore, I would receive only *accurate* information from that search engine when inputting this particular word.

The first result that popped up was Emily Writes' March 17, 2020, article in *Spinoff* entitled "Down the Rabbit Hole With the COVID-19 Conspiracy Theorists," which begins as follows:

> Today I fell down a rabbit hole of rabid Trump supporters who are convinced COVID-19 is both a hoax and also Trump's greatest moment as president. He has acted decisively apparently, while also knowing that COVID-19 is a Hollywood Liberal Elite cover-up [...]. Adrenochrome is a drug for the liberal elite of Hollywood made from actual human brain stem containing hormones from the adrenal gland. Hillary Clinton manufactures this drug by torturing children in a pizza shop [...]. Tom Hanks is addicted to Adrenochrome and he caught COVID-19 from the latest batch of tainted Adrenochrome that came through Celine Dion who is a high priestess from the Church of Satan. She is well-versed in poison as she's been lacing her children's clothing line with a chemical that makes our children "gender neutral." Tom Hanks signalled to the Hollywood Liberal Elite Cabal DeepState in his Golden Globes acceptance speech that there would be a shortage of Adrenochrome. Ellen has closed her studio audience because she's addicted as well.[7]

After reading this article in its entirety, I emailed my friend and pointed out that when I put his advice to the test and googled "Adrenochrome," the first article that popped up sardonically tore the entire conspiracy theory to shreds. How did this jibe with the notion that Trump-supporting "white hats" had *total* control over Google?

I received no direct answer to this question. I was told, instead, to search the name "Rachel Chandler." This would somehow answer *everything*. Bypassing those pesky "white hats" at Google, I decided to use a different search engine called Millionshort, and almost immediately found a March 22, 2019, *Daily Dot* article entitled "QAnon Is Attacking a Random Woman in a Disturbing and Dangerous Way," which detailed how QAnon posts had become strangely focused on a photographer and casting director named Rachel Chandler, who is part of the newspaper-owning Chandler family but has no visible political footprint and is not otherwise a public figure:

> Q made a seemingly endless stream of posts referencing Chandler, insinuating that she took a 2017 picture of Bill Clinton and registered child sex offender Jeffrey Epstein (whose light prison sentence handed down by current Trump cabinet official Alexander Acosta is currently under investigation) hanging out together in a pool.
>
> Beyond that, QAnon accused Chandler of "procuring" "girls" for Epstein, having her photography studio funded by elite Satanists who used it for rituals, flaunting Epstein's "sex and torture room victims" with her pictures, having a link to a still-unexplained (yet supposedly horrific) event at the Standard Hotel in West Hollywood [...].
>
> To be clear, Chandler has not been accused of any wrongdoing by any law enforcement agency [...]. There's no evidence she took the pool picture that QAnon claims proves she's linked to Epstein, and it doesn't even feature him— though it does feature George Nader, the convicted pedophile who's providing evidence in the Mueller investigation

regarding President Donald Trump's link to meetings with Russian officials.

And yet, Chandler's name has been dragged into the conspiracy so completely that the first page of a Google search shows nothing but QAnon-related content, while five of the top six videos that come up when searching her name are by QAnon acolytes.[8]

None of the many videos and speculations posted by Q and his/her/their numerous supporters provide any definitive links between Chandler and Jeffrey Epstein, yet somehow this red herring has received intense focus from thousands of amateur detectives, most of whom no doubt have a sincere desire to get to "the truth."

One might argue—as does Emily Writes in her above-mentioned *Spinoff* article—that when "people feel like they have no control over their lives—like in the midst of a global pandemic—the comforting certainty of conspiracy theories seems increasingly attractive."[9] One might also argue that racism, xenophobia, and (perhaps most deadly of all) *neophobia* fuel the interest in such theories. But I think these explanations, while partially valid, ignore the heartmeat core of the real issue plaguing America at this moment.

The real problem is that genuine conspiracies are unfolding before our eyes every day, but when the mainstream media avoids reporting on such conspiracies—for a whole variety of reasons, the main one being that it's simply easier to get paid slapping one's byline on rewritten corporate press releases than to actually put one's reputation on the line by tackling a plethora of inconvenient truths—it becomes necessary for average people to fill in the gaps on their own. These people may be ignorant, but they're not stupid. They know instinctively that they're being victimized by blatant lies every day. So, with no training whatsoever, they perform "research" on their own by scouring through a multiplicity of such "reliable" online sources as 4chan, 8chan, 8kun and Reddit.

Award-winning science fiction writer Cory Doctorow wrote in May of 2020:

> [W]hy is it so easy to find people who want to believe in conspiracies[?] My answer: because so many of the things that have traumatized so many people ARE conspiracies.
>
> The opioid epidemic was a conspiracy between rich families like the Sacklers and regulators who rotate in and out of industry. The 737 crisis was caused by Boeing's conspiracy to cut corners and aviation regulators' conspiracy to allow aerospace to regulate itself.
>
> Senators conspire to liquidate their positions ahead of coronavirus lockdown, well-heeled multinationals conspire to get 94.5% of the "small business" PPP fund, Big Tech conspires to fix wages with illegal collusion while fast food franchises do the same with noncompetes.
>
> In a world of constant real conspiracy scandals that destroy lives and the planet, conspiracy theories take on real explanatory power.[10]

Everything Doctorow says here is true; however, we rarely apply such clinical observations to people *we know personally.* Often, we use such explanations to dismiss the cockeyed beliefs of peculiar strangers encountered online. Before March of 2020, I had known my friend to be a rational person with a fair amount of real-world experience and common sense, not someone who would be swayed easily by illogical rhetoric or over-the-top nonsense. On the other hand, I hadn't been in close contact with him since the last presidential election and the birth of Q, who emerged from internet obscurity in October of 2017. This was, coincidentally, the same time period when Trump's approval ratings had reached a "near-record low."[11] (The full effect of QAnon on Trump's approval ratings since October of 2017 has not yet been studied in any substantial way.)

After about four weeks had passed, I emailed my friend and asked him a few more questions about QAnon, trying to understand how anyone could believe so many unsubstantiated claims with so little skepticism. Surely, I thought, there must be something at least *halfway* reasonable to back up these outrageous statements. I needed to know the source so I could evaluate the claims myself. On May 3, I sent him the following email:

> *I'm trying to wrap my head around this whole QAnon thing, so maybe you can help me. I have a few questions.*
>
> *Why would the United States military be "cleaning out" covert underground bases when they're the ones who built the bases in the first place? Who else but the U.S. military would be in charge of massive underground bases built on U.S. soil?*
>
> *Why would Trump be interested in implementing free energy? Isn't he trying to revive the coal industry? It would seem to me that free energy would undermine all of his business interests.*
>
> *According to most reliable sources, censorship on Google seems to be alive and well at the moment, which is nothing new. (In my experience, I've found that millionshort.com is a far better search engine tool.)*
>
> *I'm not certain that "white hats" exist in our current political situation. Perhaps "black hats," "slightly-less-black hats," and "gray hats" would be more accurate terms?*
>
> *Didn't the whole concept of "Adrenochrome" being harvested from live human beings originate with Hunter S. Thompson— as a satirical concept? I always thought that passage in* Fear and

Loathing in Las Vegas *was intended as a joke. Is QAnon claiming that Hunter S. Thompson had "insider knowledge" when he wrote the book?*

The next day, my friend responded to my questions with another question: "You're a researcher. Why are you playing D.U.M.B.?" That was it. Nothing else.

Since I had no idea why he had written the word "dumb" as an acronym, I replied, "I'm not playing 'D.U.M.B.' I honestly don't know the answers to those questions. I'm trying to understand the proposed scenario. If you have the answers, I'd love to hear them."

Later that day, he wrote me back and explained that "D.U.M.B." stood for "Deep Underground Military Bases." The explanation rendered the first message even more confusing than before. (How could I possibly be playing "Deep Underground Military Bases"? I resisted the urge to ask him to elucidate further, as I suspected the response would just add further to my befuddlement.) He sent me several links as well, despite the fact that a month earlier he had insisted that there *were no links* he could possibly send to me. He never bothered to explain how or why this situation had changed during the past four weeks.

Inevitably, the first link led me to Q's posts. Most of these posts were so cryptic, they didn't answer any of my questions.

Addressing my question about Donald Trump delivering free energy to the American people, my friend responded, "President Trump's uncle John was asked by the F.B.I. to investigate Nikola Tesla's papers." This terse sentence was then followed by a link to an Aug. 2, 2017, post at Heavy.com entitled "John Trump, Donald's Uncle: 5 Fast Facts You Need to Know." Right after the link, my friend wrote, "And you wonder where I come up with free energy for the nation in the future."

Nothing in the Heavy.com post suggested that Donald Trump was working on delivering free energy to the United States during his second term in office.

Attempting to address one of my other questions, he wrote, "If Google's censorship is on, then why, when you search 'Rachel Chandler,' you get all of this information about her?"

Of course, this is a perfect example of "circular reasoning." Everything Q says about Rachel Chandler is true because, when you google "Rachel Chandler," all of Q's posts pop up. So, therefore, everything Q said about Rachel Chandler is true. (If A, then B. If B, then A. Or perhaps I should say, "If Q, then Q. If Q, then Q.")

To answer my other questions, he sent me links to three different YouTube videos, one of which dealt with the untold story of the Deep Underground Military Bases.

The first video (entitled "The Underground War, Happening Now") features a "Christian Patriot" named "Rick B2T" in conversation with an anonymous fellow calling himself only "Gene." I subjected myself to thirty-eight minutes and sixteen seconds of unsubstantiated rumors about U.S. Christian soldiers battling demon-worshipping members of the Illuminati in deep underground bases.

This directed me to an even more convoluted YouTube video entitled "1 of 2—Best of 'Underground War Details! Part 8'—Gene Decode—B2T Show," in which I learned that Gene had decided to risk his life going public with these dangerous secrets because, one fateful day, God had contacted Gene and expressly told him, "This information *has* to come out!" At this point, Gene teamed up with an anonymous former "Canadian military officer" to reveal the disturbing truths about these "Deep Underground Military Bases" where (and this is a direct quote) "animal and human sacrifices nourish the bowels of creatures—in other words, we're talking demonic, terrible *things* that inhabited Earth long before Man arrived [...]."

After this startling revelation, Gene elaborated on the scenario further: "The New World Order is in the final stages—that is, they *were*, until Trump came along—the final stages of their satanic plan to reduce the current world population by 80 to 90 percent [...]. If it weren't for Trump, most of us would not be listening to *anything* right now." [Gene chuckles darkly.] "Instead of the Word of Christ, you'd be listening to the angels."[12]

As of May 28, only ten days after being posted, this video had already received 33,105 views and only *thirty-four* dislikes. (I've seen YouTube videos of random kids opening birthday presents get more dislikes than that.) The Blessed To Teach YouTube channel has over 92,000 subscribers.

If it's not clear to you yet, let me spell this out: Even as you're reading these words, there are *thousands* of "Christian Patriots" living in the United States who sincerely believe that Donald Trump *saved them from being eaten by demons* when he entered the White House. This is not hyperbole. This is a literal interpretation of what they believe.

This is the mentality you're dealing with. No amount of logic, common sense or reason can combat such convoluted delusions. These people are clearly the product of incessant brainwashing, and yet they think *everyone else* in the country is mind-controlled to such an extreme degree that people who do not support Trump are either A) soulless demon-worshippers or B) poor unfortunates incapable of understanding the obvious truths being unveiled by geniuses like "Rick B2T" and his pal "Gene." On Nov. 18, 1978, hundreds of "True Believers" in Guyana held similar beliefs . . . only seconds before being served a gullet full of grape Kool-Aid.

1. WHITE HATS/BLACK HATS

You might assume that most of Rick's viewers are hard-core evangelicals dwelling in a deep pit in the Ozarks somewhere. But my friend wasn't raised a hardcore Christian and had never expressed such views in my presence over the course of many, many years. Something happened to change him radically between the emergence of QAnon in 2017 and the advent of the national lockdown in 2020. Even a regular Joe can be swayed by nonsense with a fair amount of ease.

Nonsense has always been an essential part of the American landscape, from Salem witch hunts in the 1690s to New Age UFO cults in the 1990s, but QAnon takes the tradition to a whole new level.

2. Subterranean Wars

Those among you who are familiar with the strange realm of UFOlogy may know about William Cooper, one of the most outrageous figures to appear on the UFO lecture circuit in the 1980s and author of the 1991 underground bestseller *Behold a Pale Horse*. Nobody else at the time could beat the wildness of Cooper's claims, which included the idea that the U.S. military, nefarious extraterrestrial forces and ancient secret societies like the Illuminati had banded together for the express purpose of destroying the United States and God-fearing people everywhere.

As crazy as Cooper could often appear, in almost every lecture I've ever seen he would often pause to say something along these lines: "Don't believe me. Do your *own* research. Look at my sources and tell me I'm wrong!" He once dedicated an entire hour-long episode of his shortwave radio show, *Hour of the Time*, to reviewing the lengthy list of books he had read in order to produce his epic, forty-three-part series entitled *Mystery Babylon*, an in-depth analysis of how hermetic philosophies had impacted world history. You could disagree with Cooper's eccentric conclusions, but you really had to respect someone with the temerity to broadcast an hour-long bibliography over the radio. Even more surprisingly, his listeners hung on every word.

If Cooper's listeners decided to follow his advice to fact check his numerous claims, they would have to read such lengthy and difficult tomes as *The Secret Teachings of All Ages* by Manly P. Hall and *Morals and Dogma of the Ancient and Accepted Scottish Rite of Freemasonry* by Albert Pike—and that's just scratching the surface.

Furthermore, Cooper never shirked from sharing details of his personal background: the sometimes sensationalistic episodes of his military career in the Navy, his years spent fighting in Vietnam, or the ruins of his many marriages. He was a real person. He wasn't "anonymous." It was possible to verify the facts about Cooper's military background, which were crucial to his claims of having had access to insider knowledge.

In the late 1980s and early 1990s, mainstream UFOlogists with academic backgrounds (researchers like Dr. Jacques Vallée and Stanton Friedman) believed that Cooper represented the bottom of the barrel of P. T. Barnum-style hucksterism in the fields of UFOlogy and conspiratology. Neither of them could possibly have predicted what was coming: a twenty-first century in which QAnon cultists—a word I do not use lightly or flippantly—believe that performing "research" means typing a few names into Google images, seeing Q's own posts pop up, and concluding within seconds that Q's theories have all been confirmed. Why bother reading Hall's 736-page *Secret Teachings* when you can just glance at a subject header in Reddit and convince yourself you've solved the mysteries of the universe?

Compared to QAnon, William Cooper was Buckminster Fuller.

It wouldn't take much research to figure out that many of Q's claims can be traced back to the late nineteenth century, and some even earlier than that. This is one of the reasons it's important to study conspiracy theories. If more people understood their origins, perhaps they would be a little more skeptical when they see these theories being strategically repackaged as political propaganda aimed at a new generation of easy marks.

The supposed links between devil worship among the "elites" and secret societies like the Illuminati can be traced back at least as far as the 1870s, when French journalist Léo Taxil published *Les mystères de la Franc-Maçonnerie dévoilés,* a volume that purported to reveal the eyewitness accounts of a woman named Diana Vaughan. After converting to Catholicism, Vaughan confessed to having engaged in numerous satanic rituals with Freemasons. During one of these rituals, she saw a demon shape-shift into a crocodile and play the piano.[13] The book was a huge success among Roman Catholics, many of whom were eager to lap up the most insane claims as long as they made the Masons look bad. The April 25, 1897 edition of a French newspaper, *Le Frondeur,* published Taxil's confession that Vaughan was wholly fictitious. Taxil boasted that his book was "the most fantastic hoax of our times."[14]

But even after his confession, people continued to believe in his twelve-year prank. Indeed, fundamentalists of all varieties insist on quoting Taxil *to this day.* Jack T. Chick, the wildly successful cartoonist who founded Chick Publications (a California-based Christian publishing company designated as an "active hate group" by the Southern Poverty Law Center[15]) used Taxil as a source in his most popular anti-Masonic tract, *The Curse of Baphomet.*

Rick and Gene's wild tales about "underground wars" between "white hats" and "black hats" are clearly derived from the 1940s horror stories of Richard Sharpe Shaver. In 1943, at the age of thirty-six, Shaver became infamous among American science fiction fans for a series of allegedly true stories he began publishing in the pulp magazine *Amazing Stories.* Shaver claimed he had discovered a race of pre-historical extraterrestrials known as the Titans. Most of the Titans had abandoned Earth long ago, but a few remnants of their society had been left behind. There were two types of Titans still living on Earth, although they were hidden deep underground: the angelic Teros ("white hats" who sometimes intervened positively in human affairs) and the demonic Deros ("black hats," whose entire existence revolved around kidnapping, torturing, and eating human beings). Unbeknownst to the fake-news-spewing mainstream media, the Deros often snatched humans from the surface world and dragged them down into their underground caverns, where they raped, tormented, and killed their captives in creatively sadistic ways. How did Shaver know about the Deros' existence? Because, he claimed, he had been imprisoned in their subterranean realm for eight years. This is from Walter Kafton-Minkel's 1989 book, *Subterranean Worlds: 100,000 Years of Dragons, Dwarfs, the Dead, Lost Races & UFOs from Inside the Earth*:

> Shaver witnessed many of the horrible dero torture sessions, in which young women abducted from the surface were flogged, torn to pieces, roasted, or devoured by the evil dwarfs.
>
> More than anything else, the dero are sexual perverts. Although they must reproduce somehow, they do not seem to engage in conventional sex; they [...] find their arousal in torture and dismemberment. Sadomasochistic sex was one of the dero's major pleasures. One of the weirder stories in [Shaver's magazine] *The Hidden World* was illustrated with a crude drawing by Shaver of a dero pitching dagger-tipped darts into an unfortunate young woman who had been stripped naked and chained to the wall of a cave.
>
> Scenes of sexual torture were common in Shaver's writing....[16]

And here's a brief passage from Fred Nadis' 2013 book *The Man From Mars*, a biography of *Amazing Stories* editor Ray Palmer:

> [Shaver] recalled a woman with a spider's body visiting him in his cell, offering both horror and ecstasy. He reported, "It mounted me and playfully bit me—its fangs shooting

me full of poison—tobacco juice you know—with appropriate sexual sensations of impregnation. After a time my
skin began to pop with little spiders and they swarmed out
of me by the million." [A helpful Tero named] Sue [...] had
a blind daughter with whom he fell in love. He called her
Nydia. They became lovers. Nydia helped teleport him to an
underground cavern where he saw amazing machinery and a
chamber where the thought records and history of the Elder
Races were recorded.[17]

Even after Shaver's dramatic escape from their underground
realm, the Deros continued to beam negative messages into his
head. In fact, the Deros had been using their "amazing machinery" to invade the minds of humans for centuries, manipulating
them to commit the darkest sins imaginable.

To the dismay of rationalist science fiction fans the world over,
hordes of readers began writing letters to the magazine insisting
that Shaver was correct—they, too, had encountered the subterranean Deros! Soon, Shaver's followers became part of the ongoing
saga, adding suggestive tidbits of intrigue that were then woven
into the growing tapestry by Shaver and Ray Palmer.

Much the same was done by Q, whose posts often contained
only a few words or a single image, but whose cryptic messages
sparked endless internet speculation that added to the unfolding
drama, upon which Q would then build yet another layer. On
May 29, 2020, Q posted a link to Mike Rothschild's *Daily Dot*
article entitled "Inside the First Church of QAnon, Where Jesus
Helps Fight the Deep State," in which Rothschild analyzes the
cultlike aspects of QAnon:

Since its first 4chan posts in 2017, the QAnon conspiracy
theory has become a movement encompassing everything
from commerce to politics.

And increasingly, this includes religion, as QAnon believers infuse their complex mythos with elements of spiritual warfare and Biblical theology.

But some Christian QAnon followers are taking this merger even further, using the text of Q drops as scripture to form what seems like a hybrid Q/Christian denomination.

And it might be the future of QAnon.[18]

Along with the link, Q posted the following message: "Fear. Panic. Loss of narrative control. You are the news now."[19]

You hear that? *You are the news now.*

Participatory fiction. Choose your own adventure. A role-playing game for Christians. Virtual reality, but with no goggles necessary.

To Shaver's credit, he never tried to base a church on his theories. What became known as "The Shaver Mystery" continued to be a popular, though extremely controversial, topic in science-fiction fandom for about ten years. Eventually, Shaver drifted into obscurity and began turning his attention to more artistic pursuits, producing one wonderfully bizarre painting after another, all of which fall into the category we would now deem "outsider art." After his death, Shaver left behind scores of bizarre tales from which the *real* mind manipulators—not subterranean Deros, but human beings who work for political think tanks—can plunder nifty ideas and reboot them for our New Dark Age of Unenlightenment.

A strange fascination with subterranean beings kidnapping humans, dragging them underground and sexually assaulting them recurs throughout the QAnon theories that have spread across the internet since 2017. Similar obsessions also run throughout Cathy O'Brien's infamous 1995 memoir, *Trance Formation of America*, which, like QAnon's theories, is a fascinating mixture of truth and untruth, information and disinformation, reality and unreality. At one point in *Trance Formation*, O'Brien claims she was sexually assaulted by Hillary Clinton in a hotel room. She describes this encounter with such intense attention to detail that one can't help but feel that the true goal of the book is something other than pamphleteering.

I sent a copy of this book to my friend Damien sometime around 2001. He was working as a fry cook in San Diego, and had no academic background whatsoever. His immediate reaction to the book was to say, "This is just pornography for right-wing Christians!" Since Damien had actually been paid to write pornography (for a company called Evil Angel Productions based in Van Nuys, California), I'll take his word for it. His instinctive conclusion was that Christians felt safe reading O'Brien's lurid tale because they could unconsciously get off on the pornographic details while feeling outraged at the same time. Who else but Christian conservatives could figure out how to merge sexual gratification with judgmental loathing?

QAnon's obsession with penny-dreadful tales of Hollywood and Washington "elites" raping underage children becomes suspicious when seen in such numbers, in post after post after post, in video after video after video. QAnon followers just can't stop themselves, it seems, from dwelling on this disturbing notion. Some of the Christians who make these videos will even illustrate their outrage with digitally blurred photographs that barely obscure the illegal images. One wonders if "outrage" accurately describes the emotion they're experiencing while viewing—and reviewing and re-reviewing—these salacious images.

This reminds me of the numerous times the respectable *PBS NewsHour* has featured roundtable discussions about the worst excesses of what they called "tabloid media." The hosts would lead a high-toned conversation with academics and fellow journalists about how the nasty tabloids had been irresponsibly publishing graphic, bloody crime photographs just to raise sales. Meanwhile, the producers of the *NewsHour* would invariably spotlight these very same images throughout the segment, reframing them as educational illustrations of how low the depraved tabloids would go to sell newspapers. The truth, of course, is that PBS producers desperately wanted to draw in the same numbers as *The Star* and *The National Enquirer*, but the only way to approximate that was to air the same images while pretending to be disgusted by it all.

Who else but intellectual liberals could figure out how to merge capitalism with judgmental loathing?

In the end, one thing is clear when it comes to the creation of QAnon: Someone who was highly familiar with conspiracy-theory folklore figured out how to give these retro spook stories a facelift, specifically warping them to match the paradigm of Donald Trump's America.

3. Fun with Adrenochrome!

The second link my friend sent me, entitled "ADRENO-CHROME—Those Who Know Cannot Sleep," was posted by a QAnon advocate who calls himself Vinctum. On Twitter, Vinctum describes himself as a "Red Pilled Armenian bloke from the Netherlands that's into Personal Growth, Spirituality, Psychology, and Conspiracy facts." Though he joined Twitter as recently as January of 2020, he already has more than 8,000 followers. His YouTube channel has considerably more: 206,000 followers.

"ADRENOCHROME—Those Who Know Cannot Sleep" is a nearly fifteen-minute video that contains almost no facts whatsoever. It's as if someone read and reread John W. DeCamp's 1992 True Crime book *The Franklin Cover-Up*, which revolves around reportage about an alleged pedophile ring operated by prominent Republicans like Nebraska businessman Lawrence E. King Jr. (a crime ring that reportedly overlapped with Iran-Contra money-laundering schemes operating out of the Reagan-Bush White House), and decided to toss these scandalous rumors into a giant blender mixed with 100-percent pure gonzo jabberwocky—but this time around, *Democrats* are now the evil, moustache-twirling villains at the center of the soap opera. As with so many of Q's claims, elements of past conspiracy theories have been distorted and flipped, *always* in favor of Republicans. Any allegations that reflect badly on Republicans are conveniently left out of the retelling.

According to "ADRENOCHROME—Those Who Know Cannot Sleep," Hollywood performers such as Patton Oswalt,

Ellen DeGeneres and Tom Hanks torture children on a regular basis in order to maintain healthy, moisturized skin. Of course, it's just not possible to maintain a superior level of skincare without extracting Adrenochrome from naked, prepubescent bodies writhing in pain on a subterranean obsidian altar built at the feet of an enormous statue constructed in honor of Baphomet, the great goat-headed god. Vinctum draws passages from Hunter S. Thompson's *Fear and Loathing in Las Vegas* to make his case, but can't even quote Thompson correctly, and even misspells his last name. (Is proper spelling really so much to ask? After all, Thompson's name is emblazoned on the front cover.) I doubt this poor fellow has ever read *Fear and Loathing in Las Vegas* from cover to cover, despite the fact that it's a very short book and shouldn't take this "bloke" more than a couple of hours to get through it. He doesn't even seem to understand that the book is meant to be *humorous*.

In 2017, a year after Trump's election, I published a novel entitled *Until the Last Dog Dies*, which was about a young stand-up comedian who must adapt as best he can to an apocalyptic virus that destroys only the humor centers of the brain. After wading through hours of this humorless QAnon material, in which even the most innocuous Disney cartoons are flensed of fun and replaced with dark speculations about the demonic symbols hovering like unholy specters over Uncle Walt's films, I'm beginning to think that my novel was far more prescient that I could have imagined. For example, did you know that Illuminati Satanists inserted the subliminal word "SEX" into the animated film version of *The Lion King* in order to pervert the minds of children around the world? After all, what could be more demonic than the word "SEX"? (Isn't it odd that these Christians are so concerned about the word "SEX" allegedly appearing for less than half a second in a Disney film, but don't care at all that their president cheated on his wife with a porn actress? I don't care what Trump does in his private life, or who he does it with, but this dichotomy seems to be a prime example of what psychologists call "compartmentalization.")

Vinctum's only source to back up his peculiar claims that Adrenochrome is being extracted from living human beings is in fact Hunter S. Thompson, but he never bothers to explain how this scenario might work in the real world. What was the source of Thompson's knowledge? Is Vinctum suggesting that Thompson was a member of the satanic Illuminati, and that's how he knew about Adrenochrome being harvested from humans? Vinctum never bothers to clarify. He just floats a spooky suggestion, and allows the viewers to use what little imagination they have to reach their own ill-informed conclusions.

Because I've always been something of a masochist (as my friend Damien once told me back in high school, "You're never bored when you're a masochist"), I went to the trouble of following some of the links that Vinctum flashes on the screen while he's droning on and on. From these links, I learned that Emmy-Award-winning standup comedian Patton Oswalt (who, coincidentally, has been an outspoken critic of President Trump's policies) is a sadistic pedophile who spends his free time hunting down innocent children at the Comet Ping Pong pizzeria in Washington, D.C. In the weird, wild mythology of QAnon, Comet Ping Pong is the equivalent of Mordor, the home base of arch-villain Sauron in J. R. R. Tolkien's *The Lord of the Rings*. On the surface a modestly upscale pizza joint in a residential Washington neighborhood, Comet Ping Pong is in reality the ultimate abattoir of evil in which Hillary Clinton and former White House chief of staff John Podesta are alleged to have tortured uncountable children to satiate their heady lust for young, nubile flesh. What was the evidence for Oswalt being a pedophile, you ask? Other than some doctored photos placing him at Comet Ping Pong, nothing. Needless to say, even if Oswalt *had* visited Comet Ping Pong, there would still be no evidence that the man's a pedophile. I've not seen a single shred of evidence that links Comet Ping Pong to any criminal activity whatsoever, much less an international sex ring. And you know what? No one else has either. If those who devoutly believe they've seen such evidence would only pause a moment, take a step back from their own biases, and try to peer through the layers and layers of obfuscation Q has placed in front of their eyes, perhaps they would be able to see reality as it actually exists rather than the cheap illusion Q wishes them to see.

★

Not only does QAnon remind me of Salem witch hunters and New Age UFO cultists, but this brand-new religion also resembles L. Ron Hubbard's Church of Scientology. At a backyard barbecue in 2000 in Venice, California, I once met a fellow who had been a member of Scientology for ten years until he finally woke up to the fact that he was being played for a fool and decided to turn the tables on them. This man spoke to me for a long time about what it was like living at a large Scientology compound in Riverside, east of Los Angeles. He did hard manual labor for them, like digging ditches in the desert soil, for ten cents a day. If he came down with an illness, church officials would make him work anyway. Everyone at the compound had been so thoroughly brainwashed that if you ever questioned the word of L. Ron Hubbard, even for a second, your knee-jerk response was to turn that doubt back on *yourself.* For example, let's say you suddenly found yourself entertaining a pernicious thought like, "Hey, is it possible that L. Ron Hubbard's a *liar?*"

Immediately, you would then think, "Wait a minute . . . what have *I* done wrong that I would even be thinking such a thing? Am *I* a liar? What have *I* lied about recently? Oh, yes, I did tell a white lie about something, didn't I, just the other day? So *that* explains it! Now I understand why I'm doubting the great LRH. I'm so relieved! There's nothing wrong with Ron. There's just something wrong with *me* . . ."

Q's followers rely on this same psychological safety mechanism on a daily basis. Since 2017, not one of Q's major predictions have come true. For example, Q insisted that Robert Mueller, the special counsel investigating Russian interference with the 2016 presidential election, would team up with Trump to expose the "deep state." In the first week of November, 2017, Q announced that Trump would declare "a state of temporary military control" within "the next several days."[20] By 2020, Hillary Clinton and her satanic minions were supposed to be in prison. Despite the fact that none of these events have occurred, Q never once lost any followers. Instead, these followers have grown even *more* obsessive and loyal. Q's acolytes said, "Wait a minute, *Q's* not wrong. *We* simply misinterpreted his predictions. *We're* the ones who are wrong! There's something wrong with *us*. We need to continue studying the posts until we come up with the *correct* interpretation . . ."

Like Hubbard, Q has based his/her/their entire cosmology on past sources without ever acknowledging them. After all, the Great Godhead doesn't need "sources," does He? In the late 1980s, a former Scientologist named Bent Corydon broke away from the Church of Scientology and wrote a scathing book about his experiences entitled *L. Ron Hubbard: Messiah or Madman?*, in which he revealed that Hubbard drew most of his ideas from philosopher Alfred Korzybski, author of *Science and Sanity*, and occultist Aleister Crowley, author of *The Book of Lies* and other tomes about ceremonial magic (or "magick," Crowley's preferred spelling). When Hubbard's documented ties to occult organizations—e.g., Crowley's Ordo Templi Orientis in Pasadena, California—became publicly known, Hubbard explained that he had been infiltrating them on the behalf of the United States military. Most of his followers believed him.

This same "The Great One Can Do No Wrong" attitude is prevalent among Q's followers. If a video was released tomorrow that depicted Donald Trump having sex with one of Jeffrey Epstein's underage sex-trafficking victims, Trump would say, "I had to do that in order to fully infiltrate the sick perverts who are secretly in control of this country!" and almost every single one of Q's followers would enthusiastically agree.

4. Out of Shadows

In the Christian world of QAnon, Democrats and Satanists are the same.

The hatred that Christians harbor against Satanists has always baffled me. After all, both groups ostensibly believe in the existence of the *same* mythological entities. A Christian and a Satanist would naturally have far more in common than a Christian and a Buddhist. A Buddhist doesn't even believe in Satan. The respective belief systems of Christians and Satanists are branches of the same cosmology.

Perhaps this is why QAnon's "Christian Patriot" followers appear to spend the majority of their day dwelling on Satanism, the main topic of a thinly disguised QAnon recruitment video entitled *Out of Shadows* which features conspiratorial ruminations by a former Hollywood stuntman named Mike Smith. The third link my friend sent me led to this video, a feature-length YouTube "documentary" that took the internet by storm in April of 2020. This video had received more than eighteen million views. It's a peculiar film, as it does indeed contain some accurate and vital information. Of course, the most effective forms of disinformation *must* include accurate and vital information, otherwise the lies won't be accepted so easily. The former Scientologist I met at that backyard barbeque confessed to me that he wouldn't have pursued Dianetics at all if not for the fact that his earliest encounters with Hubbard's teachings led to many lifelong anxieties being cured. He felt he had taken away some useful teachings from Hubbard. It's only after Scientology gets you hooked on the brain entrainment methods that *do* work, only after you've invested so much of your life into their coffers, that they start dumping the *real* insane nonsense on you.

Out of Shadows follows the same pattern. The "documentary" begins by sharing accurate but little-known information about Hollywood's intersection with the CIA. I applaud the filmmakers for bringing to light the fact that the entertainment we imbibe so unthinkingly often carries with it a hidden political agenda. This has been true of Hollywood films going at least as far back as World War II, and no doubt even earlier. I myself have written a book that touches on some of these same issues, though my approach to the material is radically different. My forthcoming book, *Hollywood Haunts the World*, is backed up with genuine evidence from the first page to the last.

About twenty minutes into its running time, after dealing with the potentially dangerous intersection between Hollywood and the U.S. intelligence community, *Out of Shadows* abandons any pretense of objectivity when it presents a montage of various news reporters repeating the same words ("This is extremely dangerous to our democracy" being the most memorable refrain), not bothering to mention the fact that this mimicry was the result of a *pro-Trump* campaign initiated by Sinclair Broadcast Group in 2018.

This is from Timothy Burke's March 31, 2018, *Deadspin* article, "How America's Largest Local TV Owner Turned Its News Anchors Into Soldiers in Trump's War on the Media":

> Earlier this month, CNN's Brian Stelter broke the news that Sinclair Broadcast Group, owner or operator of nearly 200 television stations in the U.S., would be forcing its news anchors to record a promo about "the troubling trend of irresponsible, one sided news stories plaguing our country." The script, which parrots Donald Trump's oft-declarations

of developments negative to his presidency as "fake news," brought upheaval to newsrooms already dismayed with Sinclair's consistent interference to bring right-wing propaganda to local television broadcasts.[21]

Stelter's CNN article, published a few weeks earlier, offers further context, observing that at the time, the FCC was reviewing Sinclair's proposed acquisition of Tribune Media and that "Sinclair critics—Democratic lawmakers and some of the company's Republican rivals—have alleged that the FCC has given Sinclair preferential treatment." The scripted promos sent to all Sinclair stations, Stelter wrote, "show how the company wants to position itself in local markets from coast to coast":

> The instructions to local stations say that the promos "should play using news time, not commercial time [. . .]. Please produce the attached scripts exactly as they are written [. . .]. This copy has been thoroughly tested and speaks to our Journalistic Responsibility as advocates to seek the truth on behalf of the audience."
>
> The promos begin with one or two anchors introducing themselves and saying "I'm [we are] extremely proud of the quality, balanced journalism that [proper news brand name of local station] produces. But I'm [we are] concerned about the troubling trend of irresponsible, one sided news stories plaguing our country."
>
> Then the media bashing begins.
>
> "The sharing of biased and false news has become all too common on social media," the script says. "More alarming, national media outlets are publishing these same fake stories without checking facts first. Unfortunately, some members of the national media are using their platforms to push their own personal bias and agenda to control 'exactly

what people think' . . . This is extremely dangerous to our democracy."[22]

The fact that the filmmakers present this montage in *Out of Shadows* with no context whatsoever, then spend the rest of the "documentary" promulgating far-right conspiracy theories, is extremely disingenuous, to say the least. Ironically, the main message of *Out of Shadows* could be summarized as a call to question authority because what we see in the media is driven by a hidden agenda. Unbeknownst to most of the people who saw it, *Out of Shadows* is a perfect example of that very manipulation. Among corporations and intelligence agencies—not to mention certain high-profile political figures—it's standard operating procedure to accuse your opponents of offenses you yourself are committing. The filmmakers of *Out of Shadows* take this tactic to heart. This is a consistent strategy used by the QAnon cultists, as when they fret about "black hats" locking helpless children in cages despite the fact that the only government agents known to have committed such acts against children (i.e., immigrant children) are the Homeland Security agents carrying out the policies of Donald Trump[23], the very man QAnon claims is working hard behind the scenes to *free* abused children from subterranean cages. (In a world that still contained nuance and humor, I suppose one might call this "irony." In our current situation, however, we'll just have to call it a "fact" and leave it at that.)

After the montage, the filmmakers present genuine information about such insidious U.S. intelligence programs as MK-ULTRA and Operation Paperclip. Veteran conspiracy theorists will find no surprises here, but this might be educational for viewers who have never been exposed to this information. The filmmakers use the CIA's longstanding involvement with mind control programs to segue awkwardly into a six-minute segment about the late Lt. Col. Michael Aquino, co-author of an infamous 1981 military paper about the future of psychological warfare operations entitled "From PSYOP to MindWar: The Psychology of Victory," in which Aquino and his collaborators discuss psychological operations (PSYOPs) and offer up such blatantly authoritarian statements as the following:

> In its strategic context, MindWar must reach out to friends, enemies, and neutrals alike across the globe—neither through the primitive "battlefield" leaflets and loudspeakers of PSYOP nor through the media possessed by the United States which have the capabilities to reach virtually all people on the face of the Earth.
>
> These media are, of course, the *electronic* media—television and radio. State of the art developments in satellite communication, video recording techniques, and laser and optical transmission of broadcasters make possible a penetration of the minds of the world such as would have been inconceivable just a few years ago. Like the sword Excalibur, we have but to reach out and seize this tool; and it can transform the world for us if we have but the courage and the integrity to guide civilization with it. If we do not accept Excalibur, then we relinquish our ability to inspire foreign cultures with our morality. If they then devise moralities unsatisfactory to us, we have no choice but to fight them on a more brutish level.
>
> MindWar must target *all* participants if it is to be effective. It must not only weaken the enemy; it must strengthen the United States. It strengthens the United States by denying enemy propaganda access to our people [. . .].[24]

In case it's not obvious, that last sentence is a blatant violation of the Bill of Rights and the First Amendment. After all, is there an agreed upon definition of "enemy propaganda?" Who decides what is "enemy propaganda" and what isn't?

Aquino's story will be old news to viewers well-versed in these areas, but the vast majority of those who saw this video had probably never heard of him, nor had known that a High Priest of a satanic church called the Temple of Set had served as a U.S. intelligence officer in Special Forces, Psychological Operations for many years. The filmmakers imply that Aquino's existence is some deep, dark secret of the U.S. military, when in fact the lieutenant colonel flaunted his satanic affiliations for decades. He even appeared on a 1988 episode of Oprah Winfrey's show alongside his wife, Lilith.

Keep in mind that the documentary began with the intent to prove that Hollywood is a propaganda tool. So why spend so much time talking about an oddball military officer who published a disturbing paper nearly forty years ago? Other than his brief appearance with Oprah, Aquino had no known connections to Hollywood.

From Aquino, we then segue back to more or less accurate information about MK-ULTRA, interspersed with wrong-headed analyses of supposed satanic symbols embedded in pop culture that harken back to the height of the "satanic panic" of the 1980s. Perhaps you remember such delightfully stupid moments in American history as when Procter & Gamble was accused of slipping demonic symbols into their "man in the moon" logo (devil horns hidden atop Moon Man's head, three sixes in the curlicues of Moon Man's beard, and—choke! gasp!—thirteen stars twinkling in the background), and when televangelists insisted that Mighty Mouse was imbibing the devil's drug, cocaine, because he was seen sniffing an animated flower in a single frame of a Ralph Bakshi Saturday-morning cartoon.

The filmmakers of *Out of Shadows* seem particularly bothered by innocuous music videos featuring the likes of Lady Gaga and Katy Perry. In the case of the latter, the documentary suggests that only the complex machinations of dark and sinister forces could explain Perry's rise to superstardom after abandoning her original Christian-gospel orientation and reshaping herself into a double-platinum pop star. It doesn't occur to the filmmakers for even a moment that Perry's decision might have been influenced by the simple fact that the marketplace for a Christian gospel singer isn't nearly as large as that of a scantily clad, quirky pop singer. (Apparently, this is one of those rare instances in which faith in the fairness of free-market economics has failed the conservative Christian community.)

Most of what these people perceive to be "satanic symbols" are nothing of the kind. In *Hollywood Haunts the World*, I deal with the plethora of esoteric symbolism woven into numerous films and television shows, from Victor Sjöström's *The Phantom Carriage* in 1921 all the way to Matt Shakman's *WandaVision* in 2021. Very few of these hermetic films or television shows could be described as "satanic" in nature. In my first book, *Cryptoscatology*, commenting on Alex Jones' 2000 documentary, *Dark Secrets Inside Bohemian Grove*, I wrote that Jones' biggest weakness was the typical "Christian tendency to confuse paganism with Satanism."[25]

Indeed, Christians often confuse hermeticism with Satanism. They confuse esotericism with Satanism. They confuse Freemasonry with Satanism. They confuse spiritualism with Satanism. They confuse Mormonism with Satanism. They confuse homosexuality with Satanism. They confuse Dungeons & Dragons and Procter & Gamble and Mighty Mouse and comic books and pop music and cocaine with Satanism. When anything that is *other* or *different* or *unfamiliar* is confused with Satanism, you're going to experience a great deal of bewilderment. And then you panic and begin making YouTube documentaries that end up containing about 15 percent truth and 85 percent disinformation. That vitally important 15 percent keeps a lot of eyes on the screen for the duration of the documentary. But the 85 percent is the real reason you made it, isn't it?

While suffering through this 118-minute piece of QAnon propaganda disguised as anti-Hollywood/anti-government propaganda, I was struck by the fact that I could easily make the filmmakers' case for them far better than they were doing themselves. If they really wanted to connect government conspiracies to Satanism, why not go *beyond* Aquino? Why not mention Louis Tackwood, for example?

What follow are relevant passages from Alex Constantine's 1993 book, *Blood, Carnage and the Agent Provocateur:*

> In 1971, Lee Smith, an ex-convict from the California Men's Colony, testified before Congress that he'd been paid to foment prison unrest. He'd been instructed by authorities to blame "Marxist revolutionary forces" for stirring up the violence. Afterward, conditions at the penal colony worsened [. . .].
>
> [Louis] Tackwood, who'd been recruited by [the LAPD's Criminal Conspiracy Section] to provoke prison riots, blew the whistle in 1971, charging that the secret LAPD unit had been "set up on the same basis as the CIA" [. . .].
>
> Tackwood pulled LAPD skeletons out of the closet with the publication of *The Glass House Tapes* in 1973, including the disclosure that the department had about 125 provocateurs on the payroll. Some in the press, not many, asked questions. Liberal community groups in Los Angeles, discovering they'd been infiltrated, sued the LAPD. CCS [Criminal Conspiracy Section], the secret police unit, was disbanded,

its spies and provocateurs reassigned. In its place evolved the OCID [Organized Crime Intelligence Division], which incidentally maintains no files on organized crime. The OCID does, however, keep extensive files on local politicians and private citizens [. . .].[26]

One of the most controversial aspects of *The Glass House Tapes* was Tackwood's claim that the Los Angeles Police Department, in concert with various U.S. intelligence agencies, was using satanic cults in California for the purposes of blackmailing and brainwashing high-profile initiates. I find it ironic that this scenario has now been embraced by the right wing, when back in the early 1970s the only people talking about this were far-left radicals like the members of the Citizens Research and Investigation Committee, with whom Tackwood collaborated on *The Glass House Tapes*. Subsequent nonfiction books like Walter Bowart's 1978 *Operation Mind Control*, Maury Terry's 1987 *The Ultimate Evil*, and John W. DeCamp's aforementioned 1992 *The Franklin Cover-Up* explore similar themes in far greater depth, so why are none of them mentioned in *Out of Shadows*?

The same is true of MK-ULTRA and Project Paperclip. Why don't the filmmakers cite such well-researched books as Gordon Thomas' *Journey Into Madness: Medical Torture and the Mind Controllers* or Christopher Simpson's *Blowback: America's Recruitment of Nazis and Its Effects on the Cold War*? If the main purpose of the documentary were to inform the public about these topics, books such as these would be mentioned. That's the type of move that encourages the viewer to pursue further research once the documentary has been seen. As I've mentioned before, William Cooper did this on his *Hour of the Time* radio show almost every episode.

At one point in *Out of Shadows,* Mike Smith says:

> Let's take the word "Hollywood." Where does that come from? Well, "Hollywood" comes from the holly tree. The ancient druids back in the day used to take the holly tree, make wands to weave spells, cast spells, or channel spells. And when they needed help, they would consult the Magis or the "mediums" of the day to help channel their spells to the population. Well, cut to today. What do we have in our houses? We have these black boxes. What are they called? TVs. But if you stop and you say the word "television" [you get] "tell a vision." You turn on that television, and what do you get? What's the first thing that pops up? A list of "channels." And when you turn on those "channels," what's on those "channels"? Programming! They're *programming* you. They've been programming you your whole life. You don't even know it![27]

Jordan Maxwell, who's been delivering lectures about occult symbolism for decades, said these same exact words to me in Mesquite, Nevada, in the summer of 1999. I first heard Maxwell make this observation during a radio interview on KPFK in Los Angeles in 1993. And yet Smith doesn't bother to cite Maxwell. Neither do the filmmakers credit him at the end.

In the 1970s, the muckraking journalist Mae Brussell, who's often referred to as "the Queen of Conspiracies," began dedicating many episodes of her underground radio show *Conspiracy: Dialogue* to what she called Operation Chaos, an alleged CIA plot to destabilize the anti-war movement of the 1960s by assassinating various influential rock stars like Janis Joplin and Jim Morrison. Alex Constantine, a writer heavily influenced by Brussell, published a book in 2000 entitled *The Covert War Against Rock* that expands on Brussell's theory at great length.

By contrast, former CIA agent Kevin Shipp uses *Out of Shadows* as a platform to flip Brussell's theory, conveniently leaves the CIA out of the equation, and implies that such '60s and '70s rock icons as Morrison and Frank Zappa were not victims of COINTELPRO-style surveillance and harassment, but were instead the *conspirators themselves*. Here are Shipp's own words:

> It's odd because, in Laurel Canyon, so many of the soon-to-be-stars there—their parents were either in the military industrial complex or intelligence or the Pentagon. In Frank Zappa's case, his dad was working at Edgewood Arsenal where they were doing biochem studies, psychotropics, exposing U.S. troops to VX nerve gas and other things. The family kept gas masks in their house. He grew up with that in case there was an accident. And Edgewood Arsenal was doing very similar, *related* MK-Ultra projects on U.S. troops. The Gulf of Tonkin is another prime example. The commander of the Gulf fleet in the Gulf of Tonkin—his son was Jim Morrison. They claimed the USS Maddox was attacked by Vietnamese vessels. It was never attacked. As a matter of fact, they put ghost ships on the radar to make it look like they were Vietnamese ships. The Maddox was never attacked. It was an actual, literal "false flag" to enable the U.S. to declare war on Vietnam. So Jim Morrison's dad was involved in the false flag of the Gulf of Tonkin.[28]

After presenting information that seems to link MK-ULTRA mind control experiments with the unlikely notion that the intelligence community was the main influencer behind the 1960s counterculture movement, we get Shipp's implication that Morrison and Zappa were somehow brainwashed by their military parents to become rock stars and thereby create a generation of freako-pervo-weirdos. Shipp's not the first person to suggest something like this. Perennial presidential candidate Lyndon LaRouche, for example, was convinced that the Beatles were formed by British MI6 intelligence agents to influence American teenagers to experiment with psychedelic drugs. (In my experience, American teenagers don't need British intelligence agents to indulge in illicit substances.)

If you think we've now reached the nadir of absurdity, you're quite wrong. Numerous QAnon followers—far more than you could imagine—are convinced that Hillary Clinton was assassinated long ago and replaced with a clone,[29] which is merely a recycling of the conspiracy theory introduced to the world by attorney Dr. Peter Beter on May 28, 1979. Beter insisted that President Jimmy Carter and Henry Kissinger, among several other key American politicians and military leaders, had been murdered by the Soviet Union and replaced with what he called "organic robotoids." By carefully analyzing news footage, Beter claimed he could tell you the approximate time and place the real Carter was offed and switched with his robot clone. Beter's special "audio letter" containing this startling announcement is archived on YouTube.[30]

In 1992, a right-wing group called "Police Against the New World Order"—a loose-knit conglomeration of active and retired police officers, National Guard members and military officers—published a saddle-stitched, seventy-six-page booklet entitled *Operation Vampire Killer 2000*, the main purpose of which was to warn fellow law enforcement officers (as well as private citizens) of ongoing attempts by "New World Order" globalists to "overthrow the Constitutional Republic of these United States of America"[31] by fomenting various crises that would lead to the establishment of martial law. Here's a direct quote from the booklet: "Aided by their controlled media, and NWO government-paid agitators/'leaders' on both sides, the goal is to frighten Americans, of all colors, into accepting Martial Law."[32]

The group was led by a retired Phoenix police officer named Jack McLamb. Whether or not his views were right or wrong, sane or paranoid, it's clear from reading his booklet that McLamb's intent was to warn the citizens of the United States *against* encroaching fascism.

QAnon has borrowed much from *Operation Vampire Killer 2000* while also managing to stand the original message completely on its head. Instead of warning against martial law, QAnon is urging people to welcome it with open arms.

In May of 2019, Michael Swanson of WallStreetWindow .com (author of *The War State: The Cold War Origins of the Military-Industrial Complex And The Power Elite, 1945-1963*) interviewed journalist Pearse Redmond about the beginnings of the QAnon phenomena. Here's Redmond:

> [Early on] QAnon was advocating for a military takeover of the country, and martial law being enforced everywhere, and that this was actually a *good* thing. We shouldn't really worry if Trump declares martial law and the military takes over policing, setting up camps to intern dissidents and whatnot. That was actually okay, and we should support Trump when he does that. So that was one of the early warning signs for me. Not to fully go the tinfoil hat conspiracy [route] that they're preparing us for this, but just that [QAnon was] once again acclimating people to that [idea], making it seem that it wasn't such a big deal, and at the same time sucking in a lot of conspiracy people who were *warning* about that very thing ten to fifteen years ago, particularly the more right-leaning [conspiracy theorists warning us against] FEMA camps [being set up] everywhere, and now they were [saying], "Oh no, the

FEMA camps are good because *we* won't be in them! It'll just be the Democrats!" And that's a very interesting technique—or *experiment*—to see if you could do that. QAnon was pushing this idea that [former National Security Adviser] John Bolton was a good guy, that he wasn't a part of the Deep State or the Washington elite, that bombing and invading Iran was actually a good thing, and that we should all advocate for that. So, once again, [QAnon was] converting a lot of the alternative conspiracy people who have been—rightfully—questioning what's going on in Iran and U.S. foreign policy in the Middle East, and suddenly turning them around and getting them to *advocate* invading Iran and taking their oil and whatnot. So this is really, really strange and disturbing—the speed that these people all dropped [their former convictions and began advocating for] things they were previously *against*. Instantly, in the course of a few weeks, they had reversed course and basically just became Trump Republicans, advocating that anything Trump says is good.[33]

Louis Tackwood, Alex Constantine, Walter Bowart, Maury Terry, John W. DeCamp, Gordon Thomas, Christopher Simpson, Jordan Maxwell, Mae Brussell, Lyndon LaRouche, Dr. Peter Beter, Jack McLamb. Work plundered from all the above researchers has been stitched together by QAnon into a weird, sprawling patchwork quilt of conspiracies. That the original researchers are never cited by QAnon suggests that the purpose of Q—and particularly of the *Out of Shadows* documentary—is *not* to inform. It's to *disinform*. That's why there are only four specific sources cited throughout *Out of Shadows*: the aforementioned former Hollywood stunt man named Mike Smith, who admits at the beginning of the documentary that his supposed information was gleaned from too much time spent surfing the internet while convalescing from a work-related injury, which means that his experiences in the film industry are irrelevant in the context of this film; a still-active stunt man named Brad Martin; a "former" CIA operative named Kevin Shipp; and a journalist named Liz Crokin. That's it. Instead of interviewing a university professor like Christopher Simpson about Project Paperclip, they use accurate information only to drive home the real point: Believe in the theories of QAnon. And what's the inevitable result of accepting QAnon's theories into your heart?

Supporting Donald Trump.

5. Fun with Pizza!

The real purpose of the *Out of Shadows* documentary is to promote Pizzagate—and, by extension, QAnon, which must be understood as an outgrowth of the oft-debunked Pizzagate horror story.

I've studied a lot of conspiracy theories over the past three decades, and Pizzagate probably has the flimsiest evidence of them all. It's based on almost nothing except the wet-dream fantasies of far-right loons addicted to delusions about naked kids locked up in subterranean cages while being sexually abused by homosexual Democrats.

In case you don't know, the Pizzagate scenario began to bubble to the surface when the personal emails of former White House chief of staff John Podesta, then the chair of Hillary Clinton's presidential campaign, were posted on the internet by WikiLeaks in November of 2016. According to the QAnon crowd, Podesta's emails contain esoteric codes that link Hillary Clinton and other prominent Democrats with a vast network of pedophiles operating out of that Washington, D.C. pizza joint, Comet Ping Pong. One particular QAnon acolyte, Edgar M. Welch, was so incensed by these revelations that he grabbed his trusty AR-15 rifle, drove six hours from his home in North Carolina to Washington, and pumped a fusillade of bullets into the floor of Comet Ping Pong, hoping to save the aforementioned children locked in those basement cages. Why he would aim his gun *at the basement* in order to save the children who were supposedly imprisoned there makes absolutely zero sense, but there you go.

In December of 2016, Welch told *The New York Times* that "he had acted in haste and that, if he could, he would do a lot of things differently. 'I regret how I handled the situation,' he said." He also told the reporter, "I just wanted to do some good and went about it the wrong way." When asked what he thought when he discovered that there were no abused children in the pizzeria, Welch replied with the understatement of the year: "'The intel on this wasn't 100 percent,' he said. However, he refused to dismiss outright the claims in the online articles, conceding only that there were no children 'inside that dwelling.' He also said that child slavery was a worldwide phenomenon."

If I were a devout Luddite, I would use the following passage from the *New York Times* interview with Welch in a nationwide pamphleteering campaign to discourage people from ever having internet service installed in their house:

> After recently having internet service installed at his house, [Welch] was "really able to look into [Pizzagate]." He said that substantial evidence from a combination of sources had left him with the "impression something nefarious was happening." He said one article on the subject led to another and then another. He said he did not like the term fake news, believing it was meant to diminish stories outside the mainstream media, which he does not completely trust. He also said he was not political. While once a registered Republican, he did not vote for Donald J. Trump. He also did not vote for Mrs. Clinton. But he is praying that Mr. Trump takes the country in the "right direction."[34]

If the "right direction" means encouraging people to commit felonies based on monumentally stupid disinformation campaigns spread through the internet, then Trump and his QAnon cohorts have been doing their jobs very well indeed.

Welch isn't the only gullible mark to end up in prison due to QAnon's lies.

The following is from Stephanie K. Baer's June 17, 2018, *BuzzFeed* article entitled "An Armed Man Spouting a Bizarre Right-Wing Conspiracy Theory Was Arrested After a Standoff at the Hoover Dam":

> An armed man was arrested Friday after driving an armored vehicle onto a bridge spanning the Hoover Dam and blocking traffic to demand the government "release the OIG report," a call spouted by believers of an internet conspiracy theory, in a 90-minute standoff with authorities.
>
> Images captured during the standoff showed the driver parking a black armored truck across the southbound lanes of the Mike O'Callaghan–Pat Tillman Memorial Bridge at the Arizona–Nevada border around noon, snarling traffic.
>
> The driver was identified as 30-year-old Matthew P. Wright of Henderson, Nevada, according to the Arizona Department of Public Safety.
>
> In a statement, the department said Wright reportedly stood outside of the vehicle holding a sign that read "release the OIG report." The demand appears to refer to an unredacted Justice Department inspector general report, which the bizarre right-wing conspiracy theory known as "QAnon" suggests will expose the "deep state," a supposed shadowy network entrenched in the government.
>
> In a video apparently filmed inside the vehicle and posted online by far-right activist Laura Loomer, the man says, "No more lies. No more bullshit. We the people demand full disclosure."

Instead of attaining "full disclosure," Wright was "booked into the Mohave County Jail on charges of obstruction of a highway, endangerment, unlawful flight from law enforcement, misconduct involving a weapon, and making terrorist threats."[35] Threatening to blow up Hoover Dam to topple the Deep State makes as much sense as spraying bullets into a pizzeria floor to save children who are supposedly trapped in the basement.

Like the not-quite "100 percent" intel Welch mentioned in the *New York Times* interview above, the entire purpose of *Out of Shadows* is to lure the viewer into the reality of Pizzagate by wrapping this modern American horror story in "intel" that's partly accurate (e.g., Project Paperclip, the various sub-programs of MK-ULTRA mind control operations, unconstitutional experiments with psychoactive chemicals performed on unwitting U.S. citizens by an intelligence agency run amok, etc.) in order to make all the bullshit seem that much more reliable. In the privacy of your North Carolina home, while surfing your newly installed internet service, all this intrigue can seem dire and the Democrat-incited doom "100 percent" imminent. Meanwhile, if you were to use your Gawd-given brains for even half a second (unlike these two guys), you can see pretty easily that all of this is pure jabberwocky.

Here's an excerpt from Andy Kroll's Dec. 9, 2018, *Rolling Stone* article entitled "John Podesta Is Ready to Talk About Pizzagate":

> Speaking about the [Pizzagate] conspiracy theory and its impact on his life for the first time, Podesta tells *Rolling Stone* that he learned about it the old-fashioned way: from the news. As Clinton campaign chair, he had spent the final month of the 2016 race locked in hand-to-hand combat with reporters about the contents of his personal emails, which WikiLeaks was releasing in periodic batches to damage Clinton's chances. He didn't have time to reflect on the hack,

let alone notice the conspiracy theories bubbling up about him on websites like Reddit and 4chan.

Searching for evidence of illegality or anything sinister in Podesta's hacked emails, wannabe online sleuths decided that mentions of "pizza" were code for child pornography. An anonymous 4chan user posted a list of other supposed code words to search for in Podesta's emails—"pasta" meant little boy, "ice cream" meant male prostitute, "sauce" meant orgy. Soon, the hashtag #Pizzagate appeared and spread like wildfire on social media.

Podesta claims he wasn't overly concerned about his emails getting released: their contents, he now says, were "relatively much ado about nothing." It wasn't until after the election that he realized those emails had become fuel for a horrific conspiracy theory. In his career, he says he had never been on the receiving end of something like Pizzagate. "It's painful and crazy," he says. "I'm pretty grizzled. One big difference is you've got somebody sitting in the Oval Office stoking the conspiracy. That's pretty different than what I've experienced in my years in politics."

Podesta was only one strain of the conspiracy. Another thread formed around [businessman James] Alefantis and Comet Ping Pong. It appears to have begun with a 2008 email included in the WikiLeaks dump in which Alefantis asked Podesta if he would give a speech at an Obama fundraiser at Comet. From there, the trolls began mining every detail they could find about Alefantis and Comet, quickly concocting a parallel theory that said Alefantis, Podesta and Clinton ran a child sex-trafficking ring. Self-styled investigators claimed that symbols on Comet's iconic sign (which had previously been used by a D.C. liquor store that had since closed) were linked to satanic rituals. They said a photo of an empty walk-in refrigerator was evidence of a secret kill room.[36]

Let's examine the evidence that *Out of Shadows* gives us. Given the fact that the documentary is only 118 minutes long, and the topic of Pizzagate occupies about twenty-one minutes of its running time, we can assume that the filmmakers had time to include only their *very best evidence*, correct?

Journalist Liz Crokin tells us that, according to the FBI, "cheese pizza" is a common code used by pedophiles to refer to children. The image of a triangle is also used as a code for children, we are told. Let's say that's true. In the Podesta emails, he often uses sentences like "Would love to get a pizza for an hour."

In response to this, the narrator says with a completely serious tone of voice, "Who blocks out an hour of time to eat a slice of pizza?"[37]

It was at this point that I wondered if I were watching an elaborate, Andy-Kaufman-style mockumentary, but the filmmakers are completely serious. Despite the fact that every labor union in America considers an hour to be the appropriate block of time in which to eat lunch, these people are absolutely baffled by the concept of Podesta meeting up with a family member to eat a slice of pizza for an hour. (Personally, I've met with friends for as long as *two hours* to eat pizza.) And if they're *not* spending that entire hour eating pizza, the only reasonable conclusion is . . .

Yes, that they're having sex with young boys. Perfectly logical. After all, there are only two available solutions to this conundrum of what is possible over the course of a single hour. An average human being can either: A) eat a pizza, or B) have sex with a child. There are *no* other possibilities.

Not only do the filmmakers *lead off* their Pizzagate segment with this less than convincing piece of evidence, but they state it *twice*. First, the narrator asks the question, "Who blocks out an hour of time to eat a slice of pizza?" Crokin then rephrases the question, this time cutting down the time in question to thirty minutes (despite the fact that the Podesta email they just flashed on the screen clearly contains the words "an hour"). Here's Crokin again: "You can get a *service* for a half an hour. You can get a *massage* for a half an hour. But you can't get *food* for half an hour. It just makes no sense!"[38]

Only seconds earlier, the filmmakers implied that an hour is *too long* to eat a slice of pizza. This is immediately followed with the implication that thirty minutes isn't *enough time* to eat a pizza. In QAnon's coming dystopian Cloud-Cuckoo-Land, what exactly is the appropriate, Christian amount of time to eat a pizza without being accused of being a child rapist? Forty-five minutes? Thirty-eight minutes and forty-three seconds? And why *can't* you eat food within thirty minutes? I've had several jobs that only gave me a fifteen-minute break, and discovered I could consume an adequate amount of sustenance within that amount of time.

We then see footage of a former Baptist pastor named Ben Swann telling us that the triangular logo for Comet Ping Pong resembles the aforementioned shape used by pedophiles as a code for "boy love." It never seems to occur to Swann or the filmmakers that there are a limited number of shapes in the universe, and that a triangle seems more logical for a pizza joint logo than an octagon or a parallelogram. (By the way, the filmmakers never mention the fact that Swann was fired from his news anchor job at WGCL-TV in Atlanta for delivering too many reports that "veered into alt-right conspiracy theories."[39])

At one point Crokin yells into the camera, "[Pizzagate] has *not* been debunked! If it's been debunked, *explain* the code words!"[40]

She acts as if the existence of "code words" in Podesta's emails have been verified in the first place. The fact is, I could easily comb through the *Out of Shadows* documentary and claim that every time the word "believe" appears, that's actually a code word for "Hey, let's off a hooker tonight." So why hasn't the FBI investigated the filmmakers for being murderers? After all, I *said* it was a code word, didn't I? Why aren't you investigating it?

Obviously, *any* word could be used as a code word for something else. Maybe every time I use the word "conspiracy" in this book, I'm actually signaling to my cultist friends to meet me at McDonald's to lick the skin of an ancient psychedelic toad named Tsathoggua. *I* believe it. Do *you* believe it? If not, why not? Are you a sheeple? What do you believe is true? What do you believe is false? And why do you believe what you believe?

6. Successful People Are Satanists

The makers of *Out of Shadows* quickly shunt aside any useful information about actual government malfeasance (e.g., the CIA's well-documented MK-ULTRA mind control program) to make room for the "Successful People Are Satanists" segment. The subtext of this part of the documentary is as follows: You don't have to feel bad if you're struggling under lower-middle-class conditions, because only degenerates who sell their souls to Satan become rich and famous.

Out of Shadows wishes to leave its audience with the impression that the vast majority of Hollywood celebrities are involved in devil worship. If you believe *Out of Shadows*, every night in Los Angeles is an endless Satanic orgy, *Eyes Wide Shut* style. The "evidence" provided, if viewed objectively, often makes the exact opposite point from the one intended by the filmmakers. For example, we're shown a brief excerpt from Jerry Seinfeld's TV show *Comedians in Cars Getting Coffee*, in which Eddie Murphy tells Seinfeld a story about meeting Sammy Davis Jr. During this meeting, out of the blue, Davis told Murphy, "Satan is as powerful as God," and only when Davis noticed Murphy's bemused reaction did he start backing away from it. Rather than pointing toward the notion that Hollywood is overrun with covert Satanists, Murphy's anecdote would seem to suggest the opposite: Casual discussions about Satan and his powers are sufficiently unusual that Murphy found this one strange and amusing. That's why he chose to tell this story to Seinfeld on camera. That's why they're *both* laughing about it. If Satanism was so commonplace, neither Murphy nor Seinfeld would find this tale in any way unusual or humorous. Besides, Davis' flirtation with Satanism in the '70s was hardly a deep, dark secret. I first heard the rumor about Davis' friendship with Anton LaVey, the head of the Church of Satan, when I was in high school during the 1980s.

For some peculiar reason, one of the few Hollywood celebrities mentioned in the documentary who is *not* painted with this broad Luciferian brush is Kanye West. We see West strutting back and forth across a massive stage, screaming at his cheering audience like an evangelical Christian preaching to his parishioners in a Southern tent revival: "Y'all been lied to! Google lied to you! Facebook lied to you! Radio lied to you!"

Lied to you about what, exactly? The filmmakers don't allow the clip to continue. Though vague, indeterminate esoteric symbolism in Lady Gaga and Katy Perry songs are shown and reshown in *Out of Shadows*, the filmmakers neglect to mention the fact that Kanye West wrote a song called "Lucifer Son of the Morning" for rapper Jay-Z. This is a case in which the "symbolism" is hardly covert, and yet this hit song written by West doesn't even receive a brief mention.

Let's hand the mike over to rapper Professor Griff (formerly of Public Enemy and author of *The Psychological Covert War on Hip Hop* and *Symbology: The Psychological Covert War on Hip Hop Book 2*). The following quote is from an interview with Griff posted on YouTube on July 9, 2012, entitled "Professor Griff Discusses Occult Rituals in Hip Hop Part 2":

> If you want to operate in that 20 million dollar club—and higher—the 100 million club these brothers were operating in. . . oh, you gotta pay the price. You gotta bond yourself to these [Luciferian] people forever. Look at some of the other people who bonded themselves to this demonic energy [. . .].

When Kanye West wanted to be up in that space so bad, he [. . .] signed on, became a Mason and took the oath, wrote 'Lucifer Son of the Morning' for Jay-Z, and that was his initiation. And sure enough, he lost his mom. . . ."[41]

You'd think a quote as incendiary as that would be gold to the makers of *Out of Shadows*. Why not include it? Is it because the filmmakers didn't want to cast any aspersions on Kanye West? Is it because West has been such a vocal supporter of Donald Trump's presidency and pledged to vote for Trump again in 2020[42], before abruptly announcing the possibility of throwing his *own* hat into the campaign[43] (a strategic move seemingly aimed at siphoning off Black votes from Democratic candidate Joe Biden)?

Rather than connect the author of "Lucifer Son of the Morning" to Luciferianism, *Out of Shadows* tries to convince us instead that world-renowned performance artist Marina Abramović is a high priestess of the Church of Satan. As evidence, the filmmakers point toward Abramović's 1987 *Spirit Cooking*, which began as a portfolio of eight etchings illustrating twenty-five letterpress prints of what the artist refers to as "aphrodisiac recipes." This portfolio is included in the permanent collection of the Museum of Modern Art, proof positive that demonic forces are at work. Again, the filmmakers supply absolutely no evidence for the accusation that Abramović is a Satanist, much less a high priestess of the Church of Satan. I doubt if any of the QAnon followers had ever heard of Abramović or her work before these rumors began circulating through the nooks and crannies of 4chan. I picture a couple of guys in their middle-American man cave, surfing the internet while knocking back Red Bull and/or Keystone Light, when they stumble across out-of-context photos of Abramović's more provocative performances, get mildly aroused while imagining her spreading her legs for Lucifer or Baphomet or Moloch or Tom Hanks or Bill Clinton, become overwrought with an extreme case of religious-based guilt, and then immediately rush to a chatroom to condemn Abramović for her seductress ways. "Oh my dear Lord, that Jezebel needs to be locked up and burned with the holiest of holy waters! Lock her up! *Lock her up!*"

To anyone with an open mind who's not already familiar with Abramović's art, I suggest taking a look at Matthew Akers' 2012 documentary *The Artist Is Present* to see what her work is actually all about. Most of these evangelical sleuths have seen a few photos of her 1997 multimedia installation *Spirit Cooking* (an outgrowth of her original 1987 portfolio), in which Abramović utilized pig's blood to scrawl her "aphrodisiac recipes" on white walls, and conclude that she's the mistress of the Dark One Himself. (Ironically, almost nothing Abramović has envisioned could come anywhere close to the senseless violence on full display in the Old Testament. Imagine a devout Catholic vampirically consuming the blood and flesh of Christ every Sunday morning, then turning around and being horrified by the faux ritualism of Abramović's stunts.)

It would be nice to say that these allegations are the harmless nattering of brain-dead philistines. "Why not just ignore them?" one might say. But these allegations have now spilled out of the solipsistic confines of 4chan. In April of 2020, Microsoft actually decided to delete Abramović's advertisement for the HoloLens 2 after QAnon-hypnotized right-wingers flooded the company with complaints about the artist's alleged connections to Satanism.

Here's an excerpt from Alex Greenberger's April 15, 2020, *ARTnews* article about this blatant act of censorship:

Uploaded by Microsoft on April 10, the [YouTube] video was an advertisement for the HoloLens 2, a headset that allows users to see digital imagery with the outside world still in their view. (Mixed reality, unlike virtual reality, is not all-encompassing—viewers can see their surroundings while experiencing the headset's moving images.) In the video, which is now deleted from YouTube, the artist discusses her new mixed reality work, *The Life*, and tells viewers, "I believe that art of the future is art without objects. This is just pure transmission of energy between the viewer and the artist. To me, mixed reality is this answer."

There are no explicit mentions of Satanism in the video, which also features interviews with an official at Christie's—which plans to sell *The Life* in October for more than $775,000—and the work's director. Also included is a demonstration of *The Life*.

When viewers don headsets, they can see Abramović wearing the red dress from her acclaimed 2010 performance *The Artist Is Present*. She slowly walks around, and her image sometimes appears to blink because of digital effects. The artist has described *The Life*, which debuted at London's Serpentine Galleries in 2019, as being a performance accessible anytime, anywhere.

Shortly before the video was deleted earlier this week, it had been "disliked" by users more than 24,000 times [...]. As of Wednesday morning, a link listed on Google for Microsoft's page dedicated to Abramović's art redirected to a website for the tech company's arts-related initiatives.[44]

Abramović felt the need to deny being a Satanist during a 2016 interview with *ARTnews*, soon after Trump's supporters began spreading this rumor, but such a denial (a completely unnecessary one, of course) sidesteps the main issue of this cowardly act on Microsoft's part.

Let's pause a moment and say that Abramović *is* a Satanist. There's this little thing called the First Amendment of the U.S. Constitution, with which "Christian Patriots" should be intimately familiar. It guarantees the freedom of religion. That includes Satanism. For Microsoft to discriminate against Abramović for being a high priestess of the Church of Satan (if she were one, which once again she is not) would be even more outrageous than the company pulling the video merely because it received 24,000 "dislikes" on the internet.

Some evangelicals, of course, consider *any* religion other than Christianity to be Satanic. Why not start pulling down YouTube videos made by Muslims or Sikhs or Mormons? It doesn't take long for a simple fallacy to snowball its way down a slippery slope into outright authoritarianism.

7. Epstein + Trump – Trump = Hillary!

The strange case of Jeffrey Epstein is left for the very end of *Out of Shadows*. What the filmmakers choose to report regarding the Epstein affair is intriguing. Why does the documentary spend so much time talking about the known or alleged crimes of the convicted sex offender who died in a Manhattan jail cell in 2019, but never mention that the name of Donald J. Trump appears in Epstein's infamous little black book, alongside those of Bill and Hillary Clinton? (Trump's name and contact information are listed on page 85.)[45]

As you no doubt know, Epstein was a wealthy financier with endless connections to the rich and famous (including businessmen, politicians, scientists, Hollywood stars and royalty) who ran a child sex ring operation out of his luxurious "temple" in the Virgin Islands. On July 6, 2019, Epstein was arrested for trafficking underage females in Florida and New York. On August 10, while incarcerated in the Metropolitan Correctional Center in New York, Epstein won the "Most Improbable Suicide of the Year" Award after he was found dead in his cell under suspicious circumstances.

An informant who told *New York Post* reporters he had spent several months in the same "special housing unit" at the MCC where Epstein died claimed, "There's no way that man could have killed himself. I've done too much time in those units. It's an impossibility."

The informant said that the height from floor to ceiling in those cells "is like eight or nine feet. There's no way for you to connect to anything. You have sheets, but they're paper level, not strong enough. He (Epstein) was 200 pounds—it would never happen. [...] There's a steel frame, but you can't move it. There's no light fixture. There's no bars."[46]

Whatever really happened, there are a lot of powerful people in the world whose lives were made much easier the second Epstein checked out of existence. The real point, however, is this: Instead of focusing on real-world methods of preventing other Epsteins from torturing innocent children, Team QAnon wastes its time searching for Satanic, Illuminati-related symbols hidden in the décor of celebrities they dislike. For example, in one episode of the aforementioned "Rick B2T" QAnon talk show, Rick's anonymous buddy "Gene" flashes a photo of Ellen DeGeneres sitting on the set of her daily talk show. On the wall behind DeGeneres, to the right, one can see a series of horizontal lines; to the left is a mural that depicts a row of palm trees. "Gene" then flashes a photo of Epstein's mosque-like temple, the walls of which are decorated with a series of horizontal lines. The temple is surrounded by palm trees. A horrified expression darkens the face of "Rick B2T," immediately after which he snarls, "Can you *believe* that? Her set *is* Epstein Island! That is just *sick*!"[47]

Horizontal lines.

Palm trees.

Based on these uncanny symbols, one can only conclude the obvious: Ellen DeGeneres is involved in sex trafficking, just like Epstein.

One wonders how Rick would react if he ever encountered a *real* Satanic symbol.

If these QAnon people could take a step back from their own weird neuroses, they would realize that there's absolutely no evidence connecting Epstein to Satanism or the Illuminati. (In fact, there's no evidence connecting the historical Illuminati to Satanism either.) The Epstein story is sordid enough without having to drag ancient secret societies into it. These are red herrings that merely deflect attention from the *real* story, which is that Epstein succeeded in trafficking young girls on a horrific scale, and that his trafficking ring was in turn being used to collect blackmail material against some of the most powerful people on the planet.

Here's an excerpt from a *Daily Mail* article published on May 27, 2020:

> Epstein's victims have spoken in depth about his camera [surveillance] system and artist Maria Farmer has described how he had a room at the front of his $75 million Upper East Side mansion full of screens.
>
> Court documents show that other victims told officials that Epstein had his private island in the Caribbean wired up too, as well as his mansion in Palm Beach.
>
> Some have speculated that Epstein could have made his $650 million fortune by blackmailing his powerful friends, such as Prince Andrew and former Israeli Prime Minister Ehud Barak.
>
> Among the others who Epstein knew were former President Bill Clinton, Donald Trump, magicians David Blaine and David Copperfield, former New Mexico governor Bill Richardson and Michael Jackson.
>
> And in an interview with *New York Times* journalist James B. Stewart, Epstein claimed to know a "great deal" about his powerful friends, some of his knowledge was "potentially damaging or embarrassing, including details about their supposed sexual proclivities and recreational drug use."[48]

How did Epstein get this complex operation up and running in the first place? Was this elaborate intelligence-gathering plot funded by the money he made as a hedge fund manager? If not, who gave Epstein the resources to get this show on the road in the first place? And how did these blackmail schemes affect the national policies enacted into law by the politicians mentioned in the article above?

8. MindWar

The sources upon which QAnon draws are relatively obscure. For example, the tall tales being spread by Team QAnon in YouTube videos like *Out of Shadows* and "The Underground War, Happening Now" sound suspiciously like the horror stories made up by Special Agent Richard Doty and his psychological warfare military cohorts in the 1980s and 1990s. The apparent purpose of those tales was to deflect the attention of UFO researcher Paul Bennewitz away from sensitive intelligence operations that were being deployed at Kirtland Air Force Base in New Mexico, as well as the adjacent Manzano Nuclear Weapons Storage Facility and Coyote Canyon Test Area. This long, complicated, and ultimately tragic story has been documented by Greg Bishop in his excellent 2005 book, *Project Beta: The Story of Paul Bennewitz, National Security, and the Creation of a Modern UFO Myth*.

The parallels between QAnon's tales and Doty's military-funded disinformation campaign—including such oddities as subterranean battles between the American military and otherworldly creatures—are remarkable. Are such cover stories endlessly recycled with slight new twists whenever necessary? After all, why dream up new cover stories when the old ones will do? Who even remembers these obscure details from the '80s and '90s?

Perhaps the real secret behind Q is connected to the identity of the one military official who has actually endorsed the anonymous "whistleblower" in public. That lone endorser is retired Maj. Gen. Paul E. Vallely. On Oct. 14, 2019, Vallely appeared on

Mike Filip's *AmeriCanuck Internet Radio of Canada* talk show and made this provocative statement:

> QAnon is tied to information that comes out of a group called "The Army of Northern Virginia." This is a group of military intelligence specialists, of over eight hundred people that advise the president. The president does not have a lot of confidence in the CIA or even the DIA [Defense Intelligence Agency] much anymore. So he relies on real operators, who are mostly special-operations type of people. This is where "Q" picks up some of his information.[49]

Before you leap to the conclusion that Vallely is just some random nutjob flapping his lips on the radio, let's refer to his official biography on the U.S. Army Pacific website:

> Maj. Gen. Paul Vallely is a 1961 West Point graduate who retired as Deputy Commanding General for the US Army Pacific in 1991. A veteran of two combat tours in Vietnam, he is a graduate of the Industrial College of the Armed Forces as well as the Army War College.
>
> Throughout his 32-year military career, Maj. Gen. Vallely served in many overseas theaters to include Europe and the Pacific Rim Countries. He has served on US security assistance missions on civilian-military relations to Europe, Japan, Korea, Thailand, Indonesia and Central America with in-country experience in Indonesia, Columbia, El Salvador, Panama, Honduras and Guatemala [...].
>
> Vallely commanded the 351st Civil Affairs Command from 1982–1986, including all Special Forces, Psychological Warfare, and Civil Military units in the Western US and Hawaii. He developed and designed the Host Nation Support Program in the Pacific for the Department of Defense and the State Department.

> Since his retirement from the military, Vallely has served
> as a military analyst for the FOX News Channel and is a guest
> on many nationally syndicated radio talk shows. He co-au-
> thored the book *Endgame: The Blueprint for Victory in the War
> on Terror* (2004).[50]

A military officer of this caliber publicly endorsing at least
"some" of Q's information as being authentic, and flat-out stat-
ing that President Trump was forming his policy decisions on
the same intelligence sources upon which Q's posts are based,
caused waves of excitement to ripple through the QAnon community. No longer did they have to rely on faith alone. Here, at
least, was "proof" that Q was no mere hoaxer.

Yet how many of these QAnon devotees are aware of the
fact that Vallely collaborated with Lt. Col. Michael Aquino on
the very same "From PSYOP to MindWar" paper quoted in *Out
of Shadows*?

In the film, Kevin Shipp is quoted as saying that Aquino
"wrote a paper called 'MindWar,' and 'MindWar' was about
psychological operations against populations, including the
American domestic population, using Satanist techniques and
tools."[51] At this moment, the filmmakers flash the title page of the
paper on the screen. One can clearly see Paul Vallely's name listed
above Aquino's name (though it's misspelled as "Paul E. Valley").
Is it not curious that the filmmakers don't point out that the *one*
former high-ranking military officer who has endorsed QAnon
as authentic is in fact the same military officer who commissioned
Aquino to write "From PSYOP to MindWar" in the first place?

In November of 2003, Michael Aquino wrote a new introduction to his paper:

> In the later 1970s, Psychological Operations (PSYOP)
> doctrine in the U.S. Army had yet to emerge from the

disappointment and frustration of the Vietnam War. Thus it was that in 1980 Colonel Vallely, Commander of the 7th PSYOP Group, asked me, as his Headquarters PSYOP Research & Analysis (FA) Team Leader, to draft a paper that would encourage some future thought within the PSYOP community. He did not want a Vietnam postmortem, but rather some fresh and innovative ideas concerning PSYOP's evolution and application.

I prepared an initial draft, which Colonel Vallely reviewed and annotated, which resulted in revised drafts and critiques until he was satisfied, and the result of that was this paper: *From PSYOP to MindWar: The Psychology of Victory*.

Colonel Vallely sent copies of it to various government offices, agencies, commands, and publications involved or interested in PSYOP. He intended it not as an article for publication, but simply as a "talking paper" to stimulate dialogue. In this it was quite successful, judging by the extensive and lively letters he received concerning it over the next several months.

That should have been the end of *MindWar*: a minor "staff study" which had done its modest job.

With the arising of the Internet in the 1980s, however, *MindWar* received an entirely unexpected—and somewhat comic—resurrection. Allusions to it gradually proliferated, with its "sinister" title quickly winning it the most lurid, conspiracy-theory reputation. The rumor mill soon had it transformed into an Orwellian blueprint for *Manchurian Candidate* mind control and world domination. My own image as an occult personality added fuel to the wildfire: *MindWar* was now touted by the lunatic fringe as conclusive proof that the Pentagon was awash in Black Magic and Devil-worship.

> Now that this absurdly comic opera has at least some-
> what subsided, I thought that it might be interesting to make
> a complete and accurate copy of the paper available, together
> with an Introduction and some historical-hindsight annota-
> tions to place it in reasonable context. After all it did—and
> perhaps still does—have something worthwhile to say.[52]

I agree with Aquino. His and Vallely's blueprint does indeed
have something important to say. Let's return to their original
paper for a moment:

> [. . .] the MindWar operative must *know* that he speaks the
> truth, and he must be *personally committed* to it. What he says
> is only a part of MindWar; the rest—and the test of its effec-
> tiveness—lies in the conviction he projects to his audience, in
> the rapport he establishes with it. And this is not something
> which can be easily faked, if in fact it can be faked at all.
> "Rapport," which the *Comprehensive Dictionary of Psychological
> and Psychoanalytical Terms* defines as "unconstrained relations
> of mutual confidence," approaches the subliminal; some
> researchers have suggested that it is itself a subconscious and
> perhaps even ESP-based "accent" to an overt exchange of
> information. Why does one believe one television newsman
> more than another, even though both may report the same
> headlines? The answer is that there is *rapport* in the former case;
> and it is a rapport which is recognized and cultivated by the
> most successful broadcasters [. . .]. For the mind to believe its
> own decisions, it must feel that it made those decisions without
> coercion. Coercive measures used by the MindWar operative,
> consequently, must not be detectable by ordinary means.[53]

Consider this: *Out of Shadows* strategically creates a special *rap-
port* with its targeted audience by first presenting accurate—
though relatively little known—information about such real-life

government conspiracies as Project Paperclip and MK–ULTRA, then begins to push all the fear buttons to which any devoted evangelical Christian will respond (i.e., accusations of Satanism in public schools, Hollywood movies and U.S. intelligence agencies), leaves out any information that would connect Trump or QAnon supporter Paul Vallely to the "black hats" (i.e., Jeffrey Epstein and Michael Aquino, respectively), and caps it all off by ramming home the obvious conclusion: Despite what the mainstream media says, QAnon has been right all along. The final punchline goes unsaid because, after all, the viewer's mind "must feel that it made [its decision] without coercion." But the decision is inevitable. If QAnon is right, who must you vote for in November of 2020?

In other words, if it's not already clear to you, *Out of Shadows* employs the very same "MindWar" PSYOP techniques supposedly reviled by the filmmakers themselves. That same statement applies just as much to all the other related QAnon material I've cited here. As mentioned earlier, the true warrior accuses his opponent of the offenses he himself is enthusiastically committing.

In his May 27 *Daily Grail* article entitled "Civil War Psy-Op: An Alternative Narrative of the QAnon Conspiracy Theory," Greg Taylor wrote:

> Seeing as the dominant QAnon narrative—that Q drops are a secret way of informing the public that Trump is the literal savior of the world, taking down the evil cabal of Satanist paedophiles that currently run the show—is based on only tidbits of suggestive evidence and links, I thought I'd put forward a counter-narrative—similarly backed by just suggestive evidence and links, because hey if that's the standard of proof needed. . . .

What if there is a secret, far-right group consisting of an association of white supremacists, Nazis, mobbed up million-aires, and generally fascist-leaning RWNJs [Rightwing Nutjobs]—and QAnon is a psy-op they created to build an army of useful idiots, who would help spread their message so that eventually a large portion of the population would be compliant when the American putsch goes down?[54]

This "alternative narrative" might not be quite as fanciful as Taylor suggests. In fact, the evidence for the preceding scenario is infinitely stronger than the evidence that Donald Trump has literally saved Americans from being eaten by underground demons.

When I emailed my friend a brief, gently worded but highly skeptical analysis of the QAnon material he had sent me, he responded by sending me an image of an eagle soaring through a fiery Q accompanied by a single sentence: "God Bless America, Where We Go One We Go All." This is allegedly a quote from John F. Kennedy that has been appropriated by QAnon as an all-purpose motto, slogan and battle cry. (JFK might be the only Democrat in history considered untainted enough to quote among the QAnon crowd. Ironically, if JFK hadn't been assassinated in 1963, QAnon would now be accusing him of worshipping Satan and having sex with children in some random D.C. pizza joint.) The fact that my friend—unable to counter my arguments with anything remotely based on rationality—felt it necessary to respond to my message with nothing more than an empty slogan preselected by QAnon tells you almost everything you need to know about the cult-like qualities of this new American religion.

This reminded me of a telltale moment during the 2000 debates among the Republican presidential candidates. At one point, these Republicans were asked to name a particular book that changed their lives or somehow informed their point of view. Every candidate gave an intelligent, reasoned response—except George W. Bush, that is. This is what he came up with (this is a paraphrase): "The Holy Bible! Yes, sir, I can't explain my personal philosophy any better than that. There's nothin' I can say to explain my heart to all of you if you don't feel the Word of God in your *own* heart."

In other words, Bush had no intelligent answer to offer, so he fell back on invoking the Bible merely to avoid using his gray matter to formulate a semi-reasonable response. To claim that these words were mere "platitudes" would be an understatement. Bush's response was nothing more than a clumsy attempt to deflect attention away from his obvious ignorance and illiteracy. As we know now, that didn't stop him from winning the nomination and then the presidency (thanks of course to the Supreme Court). Why not? As Buckminster Fuller once observed, "Human beings will always do the intelligent thing, after they've exhausted all the stupid alternatives." Bush was just another in a long line of stupid alternatives. QAnon is the latest one, perhaps the stupidest of the lot.

The same people who wait on the edge of their seats for the next "Q" message to drop have probably watched the popular reality TV show *Catfish* and laughed at the unwitting dupes who found themselves falling in love with an online phantom too good to be true. *Urban Dictionary* defines the word "catfish" as: "A fake or stolen online identity created or used for the purposes of beginning a deceptive relationship."[55]

What better word could be used to describe QAnon's relationship with his/her/their followers? If divine intervention allowed these devout, evangelical Christians to see who was actually posting these "Q" messages, they would no doubt vomit into their Wheaties in the morning. Would they still hang on Q's every word if they could suddenly teleport into a glass-lined office building—perhaps on Madison Avenue or in the Virginia suburbs—filled with a team of tattooed, hipster "influencers" hired by the Trump campaign to comb through decades' worth of obscure conspiracy theories and rebrand them as ultra-right-wing horror stories aimed at the gullible and downtrodden? I doubt it.

In the final analysis, based on almost thirty years of experience researching conspiracy theories, I can only conclude that QAnon is the ultimate catfish scheme for the twenty-first century.

P. T. Barnum uttered some wise words in this context. (Maybe you've heard them.)

Media manipulation has spilled out well beyond the borders of Hollywood. The real battleground for the minds of Americans is Twitter, YouTube, Facebook, Reddit, 8kun, etc. That's why we're now seeing books and documentaries (like *Out of Shadows*) that claim to reveal the influence of Hollywood. Hollywood now borders on the obsolete. People are more entertained by cat videos on TikTok. To paraphrase Marshall McLuhan: When something is rendered obsolete, it becomes an art form.[56] Rather than producing art, Hollywood *itself* is the art form. Grist for the conspiracy mill. That's why I subtitled my first book "Conspiracy Theory as Art Form." Conspiracy theories *are* an art form, and they're now being used to create elaborate fictions deployed to support those in power.

We're told this is a free country. If so, everyone has the opportunity to vote for whoever they want in any presidential election. If your *informed* research led you to vote for Donald Trump in 2020, then that's certainly your right. I would suggest, however, that if you voted for Trump for any of the following reasons, you've been had:

1. Because you thought he was a devout, Satanist-exterminating Christian;
2. Because you thought he was going to screw over a secret cabal of cultistic "black hats" by abolishing the income tax;
3. Because you thought he was going to reveal the existence of Tesla-derived free energy to the world at some point after November of 2020;
4. Because you thought he was going to liberate thousands of sexually abused waifs locked up in Illuminati conclaves hidden in American military bases;
5. Because you thought he was going to save your flesh from being masticated by the blood-spattered fangs of subterranean beasts.

I may not know much, and there aren't too many words I could ever utter that one might actually take to the bank, but I can guarantee you this:

Donald John Trump is *not* going to prevent you from being eaten by demons.

PART TWO

DONALD TRUMP'S
OPERATION MINDFUCK

1. Hijacking the Counterculture

In 1970, Hunter S. Thompson ran for Sheriff of Pitkin County, Colorado on what he called the "Freak Power" ticket. The idea was to succeed based almost solely on the votes of citizens so disenfranchised that they had never bothered participating in any past election. In the end, Thompson lost by only thirty-one votes.

In the October 1, 1970 issue of *Rolling Stone*, Thompson published an article about his campaign entitled "Freak Power in the Rockies" in which he wrote:

> At the time it seemed necessary to come up with a candidate whose Strange Tastes and Para-Legal Behavior were absolutely beyond question . . . a man whose candidacy would torture the outer limits of political gall, whose name would strike fear and shock in the heart of every burgher, and whose massive unsuitability for the job would cause even the most apolitical drug-child in the town's most degenerate commune to shout, "Yes! I must *vote* for that man!"[57]

At one point in the article, Thompson discusses the almost irresistible urge for a Freak Power candidate to apply "the Magic Christian concept" to politics. *The Magic Christian* is the title of Terry Southern's 1959 novel about an eccentric New York billionaire named Guy Grand who spends most of his life playing elaborate practical jokes on unsuspecting citizens. As long as he can cause chaos, Grand doesn't care about losing thousands of dollars. Grand's in it only to fuck with people's minds, for the pleasure of the game.

Here's Thompson, bringing in Norman Mailer's 1969 run for New York City mayor as an analogue:

> The possibility of victory can be a heavy millstone around the neck of any political candidate who might prefer, in his heart, to spend his main energies on a series of terrifying, whiplash assaults on everything the voters hold dear. There are harsh echoes of the Magic Christian in this technique: The candidate first creates an impossible psychic maze, then he drags the voters into it and flails them constantly with gibberish and rude shocks. This was Mailer's technique, and it got him 55,000 votes in a city of 10 million people—but in truth it is more a form of vengeance than electoral politics.[58]

Earlier in the piece, Thompson explicitly states that his strategy was to appeal to "a jangled mix of Left/Crazies and Birchers [. . .] with no politics at all beyond self-preservation."[59] He described his base as those outsiders who wanted to "create a town where people could live like human beings, instead of slaves to some bogus sense of Progress that is driving us all mad."[60] He described the essence of his strategy as "neither opting out of the system, nor working within it . . . but calling its bluff, by using its strength to turn it back on itself . . . and by always assuming that the people in power are not smart."[61]

In 1970, to imagine a situation in which a right-wing candidate would adopt such puckish strategies for his own campaign would have been almost impossible. The entrenched members of the Establishment would never waste their time with such juvenile tactics. What would be the point? Wouldn't this approach cause such candidates to lose their credibility among their base? What kind of a deranged reprobate would vote for a candidate who appeared to be going out of his or her way to bombard the citizenry "with gibberish and rude shocks"?

Five years later, in their 1975 novel *Illuminatus!*, Robert Shea and Robert Anton Wilson introduced the concept of Discordianism to the world of popular culture. Discordianism, according to Wilson, is a religion (or a parody of religion) "based on worship of the Greek goddess of chaos and confusion, Eris, also called Discordia in Latin."[62] The core concepts of Discordianism had been laid out by Greg Hill and Kerry Thornley in their 1963 book *Principia Discordia*. The key concept is that chaos is the underlying principle of the universe.

Out of this belief grew a uniquely Discordian practice now known as "Operation Mindfuck," a name given to it by Shea and Wilson in *Illuminatus!* According to Wilson:

> Discordian atheology got more and more complicated as it was worked over and developed by Thornley, Greg Hill, and various others who were drawn into it [. . .]. None of this was *merely* a parody of religion *per se*. It was an exercise in guerilla ontology [. . .]. A Marx Brothers version of Zen. Operation Mindfuck, we called it.
>
> (We were all having a lot of fun with Discordianism. None of us were aware, yet, that Operation Mindfuck could get out of hand. . . .)[63]

Operation Mindfuck was essentially a series of nonviolent pranks and hoaxes that might, over time, upend the conservative Establishment. In a November 2013 *New York* magazine article, reporter Jesse Walker described Operation Mindfuck as:

> [. . .] a free-form art project-cum-prank-cum-political protest of the sixties and seventies, designed to sow the culture with paranoia. Through every means available, Wilson explained in a memo laying out the plan, the Mindfuckers intended to "attribute all national calamities, assassinations, or conspiracies" to the Illuminati and other hidden hands. So they

planted stories about the Illuminati in the underground press. They slipped mysterious classified ads into the libertarian journal *Innovator* and the New Left newspaper *rogerSPARK*. They cooked up a letter about the Illuminati that Wilson then ran in "The *Playboy* Advisor."[64]

In his 1977 nonfiction book, *Cosmic Trigger: Final Secret of the Illuminati*, Wilson elaborates:

[The underground press was] intensely gullible and eager to believe all manner of [. . .] conspiracy theories, the weirder the better. Most Discordians, at this time, were contributors to underground newspapers all over the country. We began surfacing the Discordian Society, issuing position papers offering nonviolent anarchist techniques to mutate our robot-society [. . .]. Along with this we planted numerous stories about the Discordian Society's aeon-old war against the sinister Illuminati. We accused everybody of being in the Illuminati—Nixon, Johnson, William Buckley, Jr., ourselves, Martian invaders, all the conspiracy buffs, *everybody*.

We did not regard this as a hoax or prank in the ordinary sense. We still considered it guerilla ontology.

My personal attitude was that if the New Left wanted to live in the particular tunnel-reality of the hard-core paranoid, they had an absolute right to that neurological choice. I saw Discordianism as the Cosmic Giggle Factor, introducing so many alternative paranoias that everybody could pick a favorite, if they were inclined that way. I also hoped that some less gullible souls, overwhelmed by this embarrassment of riches, might see through the whole paranoia game and decide to mutate to a wider, funnier, more hopeful reality-map.[65]

A similar style of "guerilla ontology" can be found in William S. Burroughs' *The Revised Boy Scout Manual,* a manifesto for "electronic revolution" written in the early 1970s and distributed throughout the decades in fragments—and in radically different forms. Burroughs' advice for overthrowing corrupt governments is the original source of Trump's pet term, "fake news":

> You construct fake news broadcasts on video camera [. . .]. And you scramble your fabricated news in with actual news broadcasts.
>
> You have an advantage which your opposing player does not have. He must conceal his manipulations. You are under no such necessity [. . .]. [Y]ou can advertise the fact that you are writing news in advance and trying to make it happen by techniques which anybody can use. And that makes you NEWS. And a TV personality as well, if you play it right.[66]

The main point of *The Revised Boy Scout Manual* is not to topple the Establishment through armed revolt but through subtler, more insidious techniques that are almost invisible (particularly to those who are not looking for them). Burroughs encourages his readers to utilize media such as video cameras and ham radios to construct incendiary disinformation in the form of convincing documentaries, i.e., "cutup video tapes" that "scramble the news" with fabricated reports produced with the aid of "a few props and actors."[67] If deployed skillfully, Burroughs insists these "prerecorded, cutup tapes" can "spread rumors," "discredit opponents," and "produce and escalate riots."[68]

Inspired by the guerilla tactics used by Colorado eccentrics like Thompson and an "independently wealthy hippie" named John Davenport who repeatedly ran for the City Council in Boulder advocating a panoply of unconventional ideas, punk rock musician Jello Biafra (the former lead singer of The Dead Kennedys) decided to run for mayor of San

Francisco in 1979 when he learned that anyone could throw their hat into the ring as long as 1,500 residents signed a petition or if the potential candidate forked over $1,500. Biafra ended up paying $900, then managed to get the remaining six hundred signatures over time. Biafra's platform included such unusual proposals as "banning cars from city limits," "making police run for re-election in the neighborhoods they patrolled," hiring back laid-off city employees "as panhandlers on a 50% commission and sending them to rich neighborhoods [. . .] and the entrances to private schools," requiring white-collar workers "at the other end of Market Street (the Bank of America, Bechtel headquarters area)" to "wear clown suits during business hours from 9 to 5," "legalizing squatting in any buildings left vacant for tax write-offs," auctioning off all "high city positions *in public* at the Civic Center," and creating "a *Board of Bribery* to set standard public rates for liquor licenses, building code exemptions, police protection and protection *from* the police."[69]

In a 1987 interview with San Francisco publisher V. Vale, Biafra summarized the outcome of his campaign as follows:

> It was a lot of work but it was worth it, especially after election night. I came in 4th out of the 10 legal candidates! Two of the people who came in below me had spent something like $50,000 apiece on their campaigns. I got 6,591 votes, 3.5% of the total. Dianne Feinstein's campaign manager said something to the effect that: "If someone like *that* can get so many votes, this city is in *real trouble*."[70]

In that same interview, Biafra described his political campaign as a "prank," but a positive one:

> Pranks planted in the right way can be very disruptive. If window-breaking is what turns people on, it's good to select

people who really deserve it, rather than just going and knocking out someone's Volkswagen window in the slums. When we're treated like mice, why not bite the elephants? A small wrench is often enough to shut down an enormous machine [. . .]. I think that what separates a frat-boy prank from a good prank is if the target is someone who has a habit of screwing over people at large and therefore deserves it. Religious, political, and corporate targets figure into this. When private property is used against the public to exploit them, then the property and their owners become fair game.[71]

About a decade ago, I had a friend who very much enjoyed driving into rich neighborhoods in Southern California in the dead of night and attaching bumper stickers of his own design to the backs of bright-red foreign convertibles: Beemers, Jaguars, Lamborghinis, etc. Here are just a few of the bumper-sticker slogans my friend dreamed up:

I never touched her
Help Stop Youth Violence—Kill Your Kids!
Holocaust This, Holocaust That, Yadda Yadda Yadda
I'd Rather Be Spying In Your Daughter's Bedroom
Window
Honk If I Feel Guilty
Abolish the Police
Abolish the National Security Act
Abolish the C.I.A.
Abolish the F.B.I.
Abolish Homeland Security
Abolish the P.T.A.
PRO-WAR (Just Not <u>This</u> WAR)

"The Police State is Now a Work of Art."—Marshall
McLuhan

Weapons of Mass Destruction Don't Kill People, People
Kill People

Cybernetic Anthropomorphic Machines Don't Kill
People, People Kill People

Organic Robotoids With In-built Photon Lasers Don't
Kill People, People Kill People

Multiple Independently-targetable Re-entry Vehicles
Don't Kill People, People Kill People

OBAMA IN 2020

If JFK Were Alive Today, He'd Be Dead

I'm a Proud Gay Parent Against Nuclear Proliferation

NO U.S. PRESIDENT SHOULD EVER HAVE AIDS!

Needless to say, these bumper stickers were meant to attract negative attention to the owners of the vehicle in question as they
blithely cruised around in such well-to-do neighborhoods as the
Naples-Marina area of Long Beach, Beverly Hills Gateway, Palos
Verdes Estates, and Malibu Colony Beach. I doubt the effect of
said bumper stickers amounted to more than a temporary annoy-
ance to the owners, but who knows? How many "road rage inci-
dents" were caused by my friend's shenanigans? Did any of them
end up getting a fist in the face or a bullet in the belly? A small
wrench is often enough to shut down an enormous machine . . .
even a human machine.

In the past, such disruptive pranks were the exclusive pur-
view of leftists and anarchists. Recently, however, right-wingers have discovered how far such pranks can be taken. But they
aren't using wrenches and bumper stickers. They're using tweets
and memes and posts on 4chan, 8chan, 8kun, and Reddit. In
his 1972 book, *Take Today*, Marshall McLuhan proposed that

any technology pushed to its extreme will inevitably flip into its opposite function.[72] In the nascent days of the internet, digital-culture cheerleaders like Douglas Rushkoff predicted that the World Wide Web would bring about peace on Earth and good will toward men, nothing but endless blue skies and freedom for all. The internet was the best and only way to make an end-run around Those Nasty Rightwing Meanies Intent On Controlling The Human Spirit.

Since the election of Trump, Rushkoff has had to modify this belief.

On January 28, 2019, Rushkoff appeared on Geoff Brady's *In Other News* radio show and made the following statement:

> Most of the technologies and media we develop are for fostering human connection. But then they inevitably end up being turned against that purpose. The big example for me is the internet. As I'm sure you remember, when it first appeared all of us thought, "Oh, this is going to connect us all to the great global Gaian mind!" But instead, the internet is used to alienate and isolate and atomize us from one another because that's the way the internet can serve the growth mandate of the stock exchange, which is an artificial system, rather than the collaborative mandate of humanity which is a living system.[73]

A few months later, while promoting his latest book (*Team Human*), Rushkoff elaborated on the previous point, explaining how the internet was seen by his left-leaning friends in the early 1990s as an anti-Establishment tool, a pacifist sword that could maim the capitalist state without the need for bloodshed:

> The original digital ethos was of a deep reclamation of what it means to be human in a collective way. We had been isolated by television and we thought the internet might provide the baby steps for us to reconnect as a global [. . .] nervous system,

and it seemed like this beautiful possibility. But the problem was at the time [. . .] it was weird [. . .] psychedelic people who were using this stuff [. . .]. It was Timothy Leary and John Barlow and Grateful Dead-heads doing fractals on the wall and that looked scary and pointless. In 1994 we found out that the average internet-connected home was watching nine hours less commercial television a week. So the internet seemed to be the enemy of the market. Then along came *Wired* magazine [who] said, "Don't worry, the internet's going to be the salvation of the Nasdaq stock exchange. It's going to be the launch of a new attention economy." *Wired* told us [. . .] that we were going to have a long boom, that thanks to digital technology, the economy would grow exponentially, unstopped forever.[74]

What Rushkoff and his friends didn't realize was that a tool created by the Establishment can do nothing other than prop up the Establishment. What Rushkoff and his friends didn't realize, most importantly, was that *they* were the Establishment, and had been for a very long time. Unlike many of his colleagues, Rushkoff has since come to understand this.

In April of 2019, he posted the following late-coming epiphany on Medium.com:

Before Watergate anyway, it felt as if the press and the government were on the same side, telling the same story to us all. There was no way for the underfunded counterculture to compete with mainstream reality programming—except by undermining its premises. The flower children couldn't overwhelm Richard Nixon's National Guard troops, but they could put daisies in the barrels of their rifles.

Taken to the extreme, this sort of activist satire became Operation Mindfuck, first announced in 1975 by Robert Anton Wilson and Robert Shea in their *Illuminatus*

Trilogy. The idea was to undermine people's faith in government, authority, and the sanctity of consensus reality itself by pranking everything, all the time.

The idea of Operation Mindfuck was to break the trance that kept America at war, blindly consuming, and oblivious to its impact on the rest of the world. Destabilize the dominant cultural narrative through pranks and confusion. Say things that may or may not be true [. . .].

But over the ensuing decades, it was the progressive left whose ideas ended up becoming mainstreamed. Really, from *All in the Family* onward, it was progressive values in fictional TV— *Maude* to *M*A*S*H*, *Murphy Brown* to *The West Wing*. And as that became the dominant cultural narrative, Operation Mindfuck became the tool of the alt-right. Is the Cult of Kek— that Egyptian frog cartoon—real? Can they cast spells on social media that change the way people think and vote?[75]

Yes they can, and they do. They're doing it now.

In case you don't know, Kek is a frog-headed god worshipped (in an ironic sense) by certain members of the far right. The movement flourished online, in the very same digital space that was supposed to "connect us all to the great global Gaian mind." The Southern Poverty Law Center describes the Cult of Kek as follows:

> You may have seen the name bandied about on social media, especially in political circles where alt-right activists and avid Donald Trump supporters lurk. Usually it is brandished as a kind of epithet, seemingly to ward off the effects of liberal arguments, and it often is conveyed in memes that use the image of the alt-right mascot, Pepe the Frog: "Kek!"
>
> Kek, in the alt-right's telling, is the "deity" of the semi-ironic "religion" the white nationalist movement has created

for itself online—partly for amusement, as a way to troll liberals and self-righteous conservatives both, and to make a kind of political point. He is a god of chaos and darkness, with the head of a frog, the source of their memetic "magic," to whom the alt-right and Donald Trump owe their success, according to their own explanations.

In many ways, Kek is the apotheosis of the bizarre alternative reality of the alt-right: at once absurdly juvenile, transgressive, and racist, as well as reflecting a deeper, pseudo-intellectual purpose that lends it an appeal to young ideologues who fancy themselves deep thinkers. It dwells in that murky area they often occupy, between satire, irony, mockery, and serious ideology; Kek can be both a big joke to pull on liberals and a reflection of the alt-right's own self-image as serious agents of chaos in modern society.[76]

The parallels between the Discordian goddess Eris and the Egyptian frog-headed god Kek should be obvious. Both were created to represent the spirit of chaos, disruption, and anti-authoritarianism. In many alt-right memes, Kek resembles Donald Trump with a frog-like face. Oddly enough, depicting Trump as a half-human/half-reptilian hybrid is meant to be a *compliment* to the President. In the 1990s, conspiracy theorist David Icke grew to fame by travelling around the world accusing various world leaders of being shape-shifting reptilians in disguise. Today, Trump's supporters (particularly millennials) clothe him in reptilian form as a tribute. They perceive him to be a cold-blooded agent of pure chaos.

The mythological role of the Trickster, formerly represented by the likes of countercultural icons like Hunter S. Thompson, Robert Anton Wilson, and Jello Biafra, has been hijacked by an atheistic, amoral reality TV star *pretending* to be a Christian conservative.

2. "Who the fk gives a poop about your opinion"

In the spring of 2020, I was talking to a man in his late thirties who voted for Trump in 2016 and planned to vote for him again. He said he knew Trump was his candidate on September 16, 2015, during the Republican debates that occurred at the Ronald Reagan Library in Simi Valley, California. At one point during the debate Jeb Bush demanded that Trump apologize for dragging his wife, Columba, into the campaign. Not long before, Trump had described Bush's stance on immigration reform as weak due to the fact that Bush's wife is Mexican. "If my wife were from Mexico, I think I would have a soft spot for people from Mexico," Trump had said.

I'm sure Jeb's advisors considered this public challenge a slam-dunk move. How could it go wrong? Surely, Trump wouldn't refuse to apologize. And the second Trump *did* apologize, he would look as soft and inefficient as any other scarecrow up on that stage. If Bush's opponent had been any other politician, his advisors would have been right. But Trump—or Trump's advisors—had already begun plundering from a far different playbook. Trump had chosen a more eccentric path. Perhaps the mystical powers of the frog-god, Kek, was at work on that stage on September 16 when Trump brushed off Bush's demand, saying, "I won't do that because I said nothing wrong," and then added (with obvious insincerity), "but I hear she's a lovely woman." To hear a politician refuse to apologize—for *anything,* no matter how insignificant or slight—in the second decade of the twenty-first century was, for some people, the equivalent of a Waterloo moment for Jeb Bush (who for years had been the shoe-in Republican candidate for 2016) and a watershed moment for Trump. Kek had begun to rear his reptilian head among the alt-right community.

Acts of chaos, no matter how small, can grow out of hand very quickly, as Robert Anton Wilson learned back in the 1970s. When you release the frog-genie from the bottle, you don't always know how he's going to behave.

And yet, despite this initial success, within a year after his election, Trump had lost a great deal of his support. His approval ratings were at their lowest ebb in October and November of 2017 when the very first QAnon post appeared on 4chan.

In August and September of 2020, in *Salon*, I published a five-part series about the origins of QAnon. Over the course of the series, I chronicled the attempts made by an old friend to convince me of an outlandish conspiracy theory being promoted by a teeming mass of rabid online Trump supporters that have grown at an unbelievable rate over the past few years. "Q" is the name of the anonymous poster on 4chan who initiated the phenomenon. According to my friend (based on the information Q and his followers had been posting on the dark byways of the internet), initiates of the Illuminati had teamed up with subterranean demons to torture, rape, and eat kidnapped children in underground military bases ruled by the mortal enemies of Donald Trump. In these bases, the Elites extract Adrenochrome from the children and ingest it like a recreational drug. He insisted that when Trump was re-elected in November 2020 we could all look forward to the abolition of the income tax, the development of "free energy" for all, and the public unveiling of thousands of grateful kidnapped children rescued by Trump's private army of "white hats" from cages squirreled away in these Satanist-controlled underground dungeons.

As a result of this series, in which I concluded that QAnon is the catfish scheme of all catfish schemes, I received some interesting correspondence via email . . .

From: Brian _____
Date: Tue, Sep 8, 2020, 1:48 PM
Subject: Commie Pinko
To: <readermail@salon.com>

Sooty you're disturb you while enjoying andrechrome. You are all sick mother duckers. You're lower then CNN. Go fuck yourselves. MAGA!! Fucking whiggers. Sent From My I Phone X

The above message is so over the top, one might think it's a goof . . . but somehow I don't think so.

I received this one as well, via Twitter:

Ron Jambo
@RonJambo7
Sep 14
Biggest load of biased kak I've read since the last CNN article I wasted my life reading. Who the fk gives a poop about your opinion apart from the [icon of a sheep] that can't think for themselves. You don't know everything there is to know. Let ppl think for themselves and come to a design.

Leaving aside the fact that I never once claimed to "know everything there is to know," how does writing a series of informational articles about QAnon prevent people from thinking for themselves? Strongly implied in this statement is the idea that the only way people can be allowed to "think for themselves" is if they're never exposed to points of view different from their own.

Here's another one:

From: James _____
Sent: Sunday, August 23, 2020 10:28 AM
To: Robert Guffey
Subject: Qanon
The 15 year old troll who started Qanon on reddit must be astonished at his success.

Mr. _____ clearly did not read my *Salon* articles, or if he did read them he lacked the capability to understand the words across which his eyes very quickly scanned. I laid out the numerous obscure sources upon which the multilayered QAnon narrative has been manufactured. These sources include such colorful conspiratologists as Léo Taxil, Richard Shaver, Ray Palmer, Richard Sauder, William Cooper, Louis Tackwood, Alex Constantine, Walter Bowart, Maury Terry, John W. DeCamp, Gordon Thomas, Christopher Simpson, Jordan Maxwell, Mae Brussell, Lyndon LaRouche, Dr. Peter Beter, and Jack McLamb. Most people outside the limited, solipsistic world of conspiracy research have never heard of these people, and yet trace elements of their theories are sprinkled all throughout the convoluted story that has become the QAnon storyline. Is it probable that a fifteen-year-old on Reddit had the wherewithal to combine fragments of Léo Taxil's late nineteenth-century hoaxed anti-Masonic text, *Les mystères de la Franc-Maçonnerie dévoilés,* with Richard Shaver and Ray Palmer's phantasmagoric "Shaver Mysteries" from long-defunct 1940s science-fiction pulp magazines, genuine information derived from Dr. Richard Sauder's 1995 nonfiction book *Underground Bases and Tunnels: What Is the Government Trying to Hide?*, and militiacentric paranoid fantasies plucked from Jack McLamb's 1992 booklet, *Operation Vampire Killer 2000*, to create the notion (now being promulgated by internet platforms like The Blessed To Teach YouTube channel, which has over 92.6 thousand subscribers) that innocent children are being whisked away by initiates of ancient secret societies, dragged down into underground military bases, and fed to ancient "Elder Things" from other dimensions? And is it likely that a random fifteen-year-old kid would have access to the White House to such an extent that he would be able to synchronize his posts with public statements made by Trump that certainly appear to signal to the QAnon crowd that the President is not only aware of Q's posts, but that he endorses them as well? Would a fifteen-year-old kid on Reddit be able to convince a well-respected military figure like Major General Paul E. Vallely to appear on a Canadian talk show in the fall of 2019 and claim that Q gets his information from "a group of military intelligence specialists of over eight hundred people that advise the President,"[77] thus reinforcing the illusion that Q's conspiratorial musing are 100 percent accurate?

No, the entire QAnon phenomenon displays all the telltale signs of being a highly coordinated psychological warfare operation that eclipses the draconian efforts of Nixon's Committee to Re-elect the President in the early 1970s. This operation is targeted not just at hardcore Christian evangelicals but also at wide swaths of the American population previously untapped by the Republican Party. The beauty of Operation QAnon, from a strategic standpoint, is that it's specifically designed to be a *secular religion*. Though QAnon has a Christian base, you don't have to be Christian to buy into the essential components of the QAnon mythology. There are plenty of non-Christians in this country who believe in the existence of demons and other paranormal beasties. You can be a committed atheist and still buy the idea that a secret group of Satanists are kidnapping children and sacrificing them to deities these elitist devil worshippers *believe* to be real. Devotees can pick and choose from the QAnon platter which elements of the story they wish to indulge in.

In the fall of 2020, Q posted a torrent of messages accusing members of Black Lives Matter of setting fires all along the west coast for the purpose of fomenting hatred against the Trump administration. Why members of Black Lives Matter would want to burn down states like California, Oregon, and Washington to direct hatred toward a Republican politician these states already voted against back in 2016, I have no idea. More than likely, the intent of these Q posts was to distract attention from something far more important. Here's an excerpt from an August 22, 2020 *New York Daily News* article entitled "Playing with Fire: Trump's Let-it-burn Cruelty for California":

> The last two years, aid [to California] did eventually materialize, but likely despite, not because of the president. Former Department of Homeland Security chief of staff Miles Taylor disclosed this week as he endorsed Joe Biden that two years ago Trump directed FEMA to withhold assistance for purely vindictive personal reasons: "He told us to stop giving money to people whose houses had burned down from a wildfire because he was so rageful that people in the state of California didn't support him and that politically it wasn't a base for him."
>
> A man who demeans his perceived enemies more than any president then toys with punishing disaster victims for failing to support him politically. Talk about the arsonist playing firefighter.[78]

In the unfolding QAnon mythology, Black Lives Matter continues to be an ongoing nemesis. In the middle of the George Floyd protests that swept across the United States in May and June of 2020, several Confederate statues were toppled by members of Black Lives Matter. Almost immediately, the QAnon crowd began sharing a meme featuring a photo that depicted a bronze statue of Baphomet erected by the Satanic Temple in Salem, Massachusetts. The meme questioned why the BLM protestors had not bothered to attack *this* particular statue. The implication: all BLM protestors are secretly Satanists. Why else wouldn't the BLM protestors attack Baphomet? No other reasonable explanation could exist, could it?[79]

For this QAnon crowd, the reality of the situation appears not to be obvious: the BLM protestors are not particularly afraid of bat-winged goat-gods erupting from the bowels of the earth to ravage their families; however, they are concerned about *racist White men in uniforms* arbitrarily wiping out their lives with no consequences whatsoever. This is a scenario that we, as a country, have seen repeated over and over again. It's a *tangible* problem. If you have eyes and ears, you can't claim *not* to be aware of this. And yet the QAnon crowd choose, instead, to be concerned about wholly invented scenarios involving Adrenochrome-addicted Illuminati initiates kidnapping children off city streets and shoving them into the fanged maw of Baphomet. Unlike the scores of videos we've seen over and over again of Black people being harassed or outright killed by police officers throughout the decades, there is not a single shred of evidence that children of any race are being slaughtered by members of the Illuminati. Instead of being concerned about the problem that's happening in their streets *right at this very moment*, the QAnon cultists prefer to worry over children they've never seen being victimized by perpetrators who don't exist. Turning a blind eye to the truth, they pick up arms to fight off boogeymen. What kind of people lead such tedious lives that they actually feel compelled to *make up* things to be afraid of?

Ever since the George Floyd protests began, Q steadily posted messages that defined the BLM protestors in one of two ways: 1) Either they're domestic terrorists (i.e., socialists and anarchists) or 2) they're well-meaning but simple-minded dupes who have been *manipulated* by domestic terrorists. Here's Q's June 1, 2020 message (posted one week after George Floyd's murder):

Black community used as pawns?
Welcome to the [Democratic] party.
UNITY CREATES PEACE.
UNITY IS HUMANITY.[80]

According to Q's scenario, Black people aren't smart enough to make their own decisions; the puppeteers in charge of the Democratic Party make decisions *for* them. The definition of "unity" is sitting at home, not protesting when police officers are killing you, and voting for Trump. The people who hang on every new Q post accept this distorted portrayal of the BLM movement without skepticism. The idea that most of the protestors are simply pissed off about hundreds of years of injustices dealt to them by law enforcement doesn't seem to occur to them. (Or if it does occur to them, they consciously choose to believe in a lie instead.)

Some commentators blame the shallowness of typical middle American Christian values for QAnon's current popularity. Here's an illuminating excerpt from a May 18, 2020 Conversation.com article by Marc-André Argentino:

I have been studying the growth of the QAnon movement as part of my research into how extremist religious and political organizations create propaganda and recruit new members to ideological causes.

On Feb. 23, I logged onto Zoom to observe the first
public service of what is essentially a QAnon church operating out of the Omega Kingdom Ministry (OKM). I've spent
12 weeks attending this two-hour Sunday morning service.
What I've witnessed is an existing model of neo-charismatic home churches—the neo-charismatic movement is an
offshoot of evangelical Protestant Christianity and is made up
of thousands of independent organizations—where QAnon
conspiracy theories are reinterpreted through the Bible. In
turn, QAnon conspiracy theories serve as a lens to interpret
the Bible itself [. . .].

The Sunday service is led by Russ Wagner, leader of the
Indiana-based OKM, and Kevin Bushey, a retired colonel
running for election to the Maine House of Representatives.
The service begins with an opening prayer from Wagner
that he says will protect the Zoom room from Satan. This is
followed by an hour-long Bible study where Wagner might
explain the *Fall Cabal* video that attendees had just watched
or offer his observations on socio-political events from the
previous week.

Everything is explained through the lens of the Bible and
QAnon narratives. Bushey then does 45 minutes of decoding
items that have appeared recently on the app called QMap
that is used to share conspiracy theories. The last 15 minutes
are dedicated to communion and prayer.[81]

Despite the growing popularity of the QAnon mythology among
hardcore Christians, evangelicals are by no means the only ones
being taken in by Q. The QAnon crowd includes libertarians,
former liberals, disillusioned Democrats, conspiracy theorists,
fans of the paranormal and High Strangeness, anarchists, accel-
erationists, and (most disturbingly) thousands upon thousands of

otherwise typical voters who have become disenfranchised from an ineffectual Democratic Party that insists on drifting further and further away from the needs of the average person. In a very real way, QAnon is the inevitable result of what the Democrats have always been so good at: mouthing concern for the "common person" while their actions reveal a far different imperative.

I'm reminded of that wonderful scene in Michael Moore's documentary, *Bowling for Columbine*, in which we discover that Mark Koernke, the head of the Michigan militia movement in the 1990s, had been working full-time as a janitor at the local university for years. Moore paints the ironic picture of a group of academics sitting in a classroom afterhours, discussing their desperate desire for social change, sipping their Starbucks Frappuccinos, while only ten feet away from their little intellectual coffee klatch Koernke swept their garbage from the floor, completely ignored by these sensitive liberals.

Just as the militia movement of the 1990s served the needs of average working people alienated from the elitist corridors of academia and effete liberalism, QAnon came along during a moment of crisis and provided what all cults offer their beaten-down followers: an explanation of why they're living in such extreme poverty while everyone else around them—half-real phantoms seen haunting Facebook, Instagram, television—seem to prosper and flourish. Is it because someone's *keeping* them down? If so, who is it? *Who?*

"Why the hell are they doing this to me, Martha? *Why?* Heck, if only child-eating Satanists are allowed to climb the ladder to success, then I don't have to feel bad about being trapped down here on the lowest rung, do I? Now that I think about it, I don't even *want* to be successful—not if I have to gnaw on piles of prepubescent flesh to succeed! Why the hell even *try*, right, Martha? The cards are stacked against me and *all* right-thinking

people. And besides. . . before I can even think about getting
my life in order, I need to do something about all them poor
kids trapped in those underground cages. Not those immigrant
kids from Mexico, though! I don't mean them . . . not at all. I
don't care about them ragamuffins being stuffed in cages. No,
I'm talking about all them *White kids* trapped inside those underground military bases controlled by them nasty Illuminati fuck-
ers. Oh, wait . . . I just realized something! I have no way of
finding those cages because that's Above Top Secret information. An average guy like me would never have access to intel
like that. So what can I do about it then? Nothing, I guess. So
I'll just sit here in my man-cave and wait for Q to tell me what
to do. And when Trump declares martial law, I'll *know* it's a
good thing. It'll mean he's finally cleaning out all them Satanists
from the public schools and the hospitals and the churches and
the Hollywood studios and the underground bases and whatnot.
Trust in Q and Donald! Only *they* know what's right for us! Isn't
that right, Martha? *Martha?* Where the hell're you going with
that suitcase?"

QAnon is the most fascinating sociological experiment
to be conducted on the American population in many years.
Perhaps it's not the *only* such experiment, but it might be the
most impactful. Since the early 1990s, a large segment of libertarians—the same kind who hung on the paranoid ravings of
such militia leaders as the aforementioned Mark Koernke before
he was imprisoned for assaulting police officers—have feared an
imminent fascist coup in the United States. For years, these people had been raising the alarm bells about "concentration camps"
being secretly built all over America. Within only a few weeks,
these same libertarians spun around and embraced the possibility of martial law merely because Q (*an anonymous poster on the
internet*) declared that Trump would use martial law as a tool

to destroy the dangerous cult of liberal Democrats, Satanists, and child molesters who are secretly in control of this country. Within a short period of time, their entire worldview had been altered. These people couldn't *wait* for the concentration camps to be established because, after all, those dirty stinking *Democrats* were going to be filling up them ovens now, boy, not God-loving Christian patriots.

So what's the purpose of this social experiment? The purpose is to distract the citizenry from the *real* problems, from the people who are actually controlling this country.

Now hold on a second . . . that sounds an awful lot like the "Deep State" model touted by Trump. Is that what you're talking about? Are you some sort of secret Trump supporter, you son of a bitch? Are you saying the Deep State is *real*?

The origins of the term "Deep State" can be traced back to the academic left. Similar to how a private think tank composed of wordsmiths, persuasion engineers, and culture vultures was no doubt hired to construct the QAnon narrative for the purposes of upping Trump's popularity, the President's most infamous quips and catchphrases were clearly plundered from previous sources, several of them associated with the radical counterculture or the leftwing. As already noted, the term "fake news" first appeared in William Burroughs' *The Revised Boy Scout Manual* in the early 1970s (though I highly doubt Trump himself is aware of that fact).

Investigative journalist Jon Rappoport—author of such books as *AIDS INC.* (1988) and *The Secret Behind Secret Societies* (1998)—named his website "Nomorefakenews" at least *two decades* before Trump's advisors appropriated the term for their own purposes. In the popular mind, Rappoport's definition of the phrase has now been grossly distorted from its original intent, which was to critique the hidden agendas of mainstream journalists on both the right *and* the left—and every political persuasion in between.

Trump's advisors appropriated the term "Deep State" from a 1993 book entitled *Deep Politics and the Death of JFK* by Peter Dale Scott, an English professor at UC Berkeley. In this highly detailed, well-researched tome, Scott offers a sober analysis of how Kennedy's assassination undermined American democracy in order to alter U.S. policies in Vietnam (among numerous other imperialistic goals). It seems clear that Scott had to figure out a way to write about complex political machinations for a respectable academic press without ever using the word "conspiracy" in order to avoid advertising the fact that this was, indeed, a book analyzing a vast conspiracy. Instead of "conspiracy theories," Scott compromised and used "Deep Politics." Trump's appropriation of the term renders Scott's historically important book an anathema for those who would no doubt glance at the cover and assume this Scott fellow must have been a far-right-wing lunatic suffering from the delusion that Ted Cruz's father had something to do with the assassination of JFK.

Does the term "Deep State" accurately reflect how the U.S. government operates? The phrase implies that what we see in everyday Washington, D.C. politics is little more than a false front, like those fake towns used in old Hollywood westerns in which grocery stores, hotels, and bullet-ridden saloons were really nothing more than a flimsy façade. The true action occurred behind the scenes. Who directed the film? Who wrote it? Who framed the shot? These key players, of course, are never shown on-screen.

This outlook borders on a Gnostic view of reality: that everything our eyes see is a cheap illusion, a Black Iron Prison forged by half-mad angels who sincerely believe they're gods but—in reality, the *real* reality—are nothing more than sadistic overlords with a weird addiction to manipulating human lives for fun. Perhaps there's some value in this model as a metaphor. But is it *literally* true?

In reality—the *real* reality—the "Deep State" so feared by Trump's followers would be more accurately described as the "Satellite Government." After all, the word "deep" implies something that's buried, hidden far out of sight. The Satellite Government is not buried, nor is it hidden out of sight. It's on display for all to see. But hardly anyone is looking in the right places.

3. The Purloined Letter

Consider Edgar Allan Poe. In 1841 Poe created the very first literary detective, Monsieur C. Auguste Dupin, in his celebrated short story "The Murders in the Rue Morgue." Fifty years later this story would inspire Arthur Conan Doyle to create the most famous literary detective of all time, Sherlock Holmes. In 1844 Poe wrote a sequel to "The Murders in the Rue Morgue" entitled "The Purloined Letter" in which Dupin outsmarts the Prefect of the Parisian Police by doing what the Prefect cannot: retrieve a most incriminating letter that has been stolen from a member of the royal family. The entire police department has searched the room of the thief and come up empty-handed. It takes Dupin to point out the obvious to the Prefect: this entire time the envelope they're searching for has been sitting safely in the letter holder perched on the mantelpiece. Hidden in plain view. Camouflaged by expectations.

If you're busy scrounging around for something you're certain is so "deep" that it's been completely obscured from view, your eyes will never alight upon the true target of your quest.

When I see throngs of people taking to the streets to protest "fascism," I often wonder if they know what "fascism" really is. It's difficult to fight something if you have only a vague understanding of it. According to Benito Mussolini, "Fascism is Corporatism."[82]

The Satellite Government is composed of *corporations* that continually orbit the centers of power in Washington, D.C. as reliably as the Earth revolves around the sun. Taking full advantage of the all-encompassing powers granted to them by the

National Security Act of 1947 and the Patriot Act of 2001, these corporations have gradually rolled back all constitutional guarantees, exploited millions of American citizens by using *identities* as sources of income, and have succeeded in building an empire out of the most anti-human, money-making schemes of the past two centuries. In the name of fighting domestic and foreign terrorists, while magnifying paranoia through the branding of innocent citizens and human rights groups as dire threats against national security, these corporations have managed to normalize surveillance and harassment as the Order of the Day. And it's only going to get worse from here.

How many hours have Trumpist conservatives wasted being consumed by anger at the fictional occultists that have evolved into the main antagonists of the strategically devised QAnon storyline, in truth a massive psychological warfare operation deployed against the American people by a Trump-backed political think tank? These conservatives—many of whom no doubt have a sincere desire to learn the facts about the people in power who have manipulated them for so long—spend their days and nights composing inflammatory Twitter posts about liberal politicians they wish to believe are Satanist pedophiles who must extract precious bodily fluids from kidnapped waifs in order to remain in power. Imagine if these same conservatives redirected their frustration into researching the *real* people who are exploiting their hearts and minds and souls and imaginations?

4. Fascism Is Corporatism

Due to the feedback I received after the publication of my book *Chameleo* in 2015, I've learned a great deal about an extralegal tactic exploited by American intelligence agencies more and more frequently since the passing of the Patriot Act in 2001. These agencies farm out to an array of private corporations the sometimes delicate, sometimes brutal task of surveilling and harassing private citizens deemed to be "suspected terrorists." Who has the power to label someone a "suspected terrorist"? Why, the people whose jobs depend on a steady stream of potential terrorists, of course.

During the past seven years, I've communicated with a diverse range of innocent people who have been victimized by such corporations for years, even decades. According to these victims (survivors, in truth), certain key multinational corporations are at the forefront of these unconstitutional operations, among them DSAC (Domestic Security Alliance Council), EKS Group, InfraGard, ITA International, the MASY Group, Prescient Edge, SAIC (Scientific Applications International Corporation), and Whitney, Bradley & Brown. These companies are global providers of "high impact National Security, intelligence, and private sector capital management solutions"[83] and claim to provide their loyal clients with "years of experience in areas surrounding intelligence operations, law enforcement, counterintelligence, human intelligence, information operations, counter-terrorism, force protection, security matters, international diplomacy and foreign area knowledge."[84]

Who are the top-level managers of these little-known cor-porations? This is publicly available information. It's not buried out back somewhere, miles and miles behind a false-front bul-let-ridden saloon, along with all that other "Deep State" data. It's posted on the internet. Sitting right there on the mantelpiece. In the letter holder.

A simple Google search will get you closer to seeing the true faces of those who are manipulating you rather than attempting to scry such "Top Secret" information from the virtual crystal balls and cryptic codes made available to you by Q on qalerts. app.

Imagine if all those QAnon followers had just stopped hang-ing on Q's every post and instead banded together and demanded the repeal of the National Security Act and the Patriot Act. Perhaps, then, a real revolution of total disclosure would occur in this country.

5. President Kek

When one speaks to some of Trump's supporters face to face, it becomes far easier to see the universe through their eyes (at least for a moment). They genuinely feel oppressed by an entrenched Establishment that claims it's one thing while demonstrating over and over again that it's something else entirely. If Trump wears his reptilian face on the outside, these people believe the leftwing Establishment wears its reptilian face on the inside. I can't say they're wrong. Perhaps some of these people would simply *prefer* to see the true face of the reptile as the beast sinks its fangs into their collective necks. This is an existential choice, one I'm not willing to judge.

Consider this example of audacious hypocrisy: In September of 2020, Trump received criticism from the mainstream media because he allegedly referred to those who died while serving in the military as "losers" and "suckers."[85]

★

"I'm shocked, *shocked* . . . !"
—Captain Renault (Claude Rains) in Michael Curtiz's
Casablanca (1942)

★

Let's pause a moment and examine reality as it exists, and not as we wish it to exist.

Is there anyone on the planet who thinks there's a politician in existence who hasn't thought the same exact thing? Given the unusual amount of politicians' sons (including George W. Bush) who avoided fighting for their country during wartime, I don't think it's outrageous to conclude that almost every politician alive today harbors those same opinions about the "common man." You're telling me that a five-star military leader points at a distant hilltop surrounded by explosive mines, shouts, "Charge!," watches a bunch of clueless teenage boys frog-march into a painful death and/or a long life of limbless paralysis, and doesn't chuckle about it among the other merchants of doom back at the Lodge meeting on Monday night?

Is it better to have a politician in the White House who buries these sadistic thoughts deep in his psyche, squeezing out crocodile tears for fallen soldier boys every Veterans Day, rather than the one who blurts out his most selfish impulses at random moments during public press conferences? Do the American people want a leader morally superior to President Kek, or do they just want one who will utter the proper platitudes, in the proper tone, at the proper time?

Perhaps the internet didn't give us peace on Earth, but it did give us telepathy, the ability (via Twitter) to peer into the mind of a living President. This is unprecedented. Never before have the American people had almost unlimited access to the cobwebbed, haunted interior of a powerful politician's brain. The experience is not pleasant by any means, but I have to admit that I get a little sad when I reflect on all those potential, unborn, pre-aborted Tweets we missed out on during the technological Dark Ages in which such miscreants as Richard Nixon and Ronald Reagan had no access to Twitter whatsoever. Imagine Nixon compulsively spilling the beans, via social media, about CREEP and his professional pistoleros, G. Gordon Liddy and E. Howard Hunt, who were running around the country breaking into the offices of Daniel Ellsberg's psychiatrist and trying to bump off troublesome investigative journalists like Jack Anderson. Who knows? Perhaps Liddy and Hunt would have gone to prison far sooner than they did (probably not).

If Trump has perfected the role of a corrupt President, he certainly didn't invent it. Ronald Reagan, you may recall, went out of his way to kneel at the graves of Nazis in Bitburg, Germany in May of 1985 and proudly stated that the SS troops "were victims, just as surely as the victims in the concentration camps."[86] This proclamation isn't too far removed from Trump's infamous "There are very fine people on both sides" statement (referring to the Charlottesville protests during which neo-Nazis and anti-racists clashed).[87] Trump's opinion isn't all that surprising, particularly in light of the fact that his campaign accepted thousands of dollars in donations from neo-Nazis, as reported by *Popular Information*.[88] Perhaps what should disturb people the most about the Trump administration is that the ugliness we see on constant public display is merely an extension of "Business As Usual." A sitting President going out of his way to arrange a photo-op to document for posterity the day he prayed at the graves of Nazis is about as blatantly twisted as you can get. Imagine the delicious secrets that would have erupted out of Reagan's Alzheimer's-riddled brain during the 1980s if social media had existed. It would have been a quasi-surreal, absurdist miracle to behold. Who knows how much information we would have been able to access? Perhaps we would have learned far more about the Iran-Contra affair than official history is willing to tell us, and Reagan would have been impeached twelve times over.

My liberal friends are constantly astounded by how many misogynistic, racist comments can tumble out of Trump's mouth with no seeming effect on the loyalty of his base. But several of the Trump supporters I spoke to claimed that they were not voting for him because they thought he was a misogynist racist.

They insisted that they were voting for him simply because Democrats *hate* him so much. They may not even like Trump. They may even hate him . . . but they hate him a lot less than those politicians they perceive to be in power, politicians they believe have betrayed them. If pressed, they embrace the label of being "anti-Establishment." These followers of Kek have identified, either consciously or subconsciously, what Douglas Rushkoff figured out only recently: In the digital environment, the "Establishment" is not represented by the people who control the US Congress or the person who's sitting behind the Resolute Desk in the White House.

6. Reclaiming Operation Mindfuck

A frequent correspondent recently sent me a link to a YouTube clip that purports to be an interview with a man who, under duress, is forced to perform surveillance and harassment operations for a private corporation. What my readers will find most fascinating about this exchange is that certain statements made by the interviewee seem to confirm various speculations laid out in the pages of my book *Chameleo*.

A choice quote from said gentleman: "When they abolished slavery, they formed a new approach to slavery. They pick on the poor in order for certain businesses to thrive financially, and as the economy gets worse, then the need [grows] for more and more people to be manipulated into breaking the law and doing things that will help bring money into the prisons."[89] In this regard, it might be relevant to point out that private-prison stock values shot through the stratosphere only days after Trump's election to the presidency. On November 9, 2016, Tracy Alloway and Lily Katz published an article in *Bloomberg* entitled "Private Prison Stocks Are Surging After Trump's Win":

> Two companies that operate detention facilities in the US are breaking out. Donald Trump's victory in the presidential elections helped shares of Corrections Corp. rise as much as 60 percent before paring their surge to 34 percent by 10:14 am in New York, while GEO Group Inc. was trading 18 percent higher by the same time.
>
> Those moves mean the stocks have recouped some of the losses they've registered since August, when the Department

of Justice said it would start phasing out privately run jails. Analysts say President Trump would be likely to reverse that policy, and see an added windfall to the companies stemming from the difficulty of implementing his deportation agenda.

"Private prisons would likely be a clear winner under Trump, as his administration will likely rescind the DOJ's contract phase-out and ICE capacity to house detainees will come under further stress," analysts at Height Securities LLC wrote in a note published this morning, referring to the Immigration and Customs Enforcement body by its acronym. Mass deportation of illegal immigrants would be likely to run into legal obstacles, "further necessitating a sizable contract detention population," the analysts said.[90]

In Rita Nazareth, Anna-Louise Jackson, and Eliza Ronalds-Hannon's November 9, 2016 *Bloomberg* article entitled "US Stocks Rise, Treasuries Fall as Trump Win Spurs Growth Bets," the authors identify a list of "WINNERS" (economically speaking) in the wake of Trump's election:

BANKS: rallied as Trump has vowed to reduce regulation.

DRUGMAKERS: surged as Democratic threats of price controls are no longer a concern with Republicans retaining both houses of Congress.

DEFENSE & INFRASTRUCTURE: Lockheed Martin Corp. and Caterpillar Inc. climbed on Trump's pledge to boost spending in both industries.

PRISON OPERATORS: Corrections Corp. soared on speculation the new administration will rescind a government contract phase-out.[91]

Ironically, Trump was able to tap into an extreme "anti-government" sentiment burning beneath the surface of American psychology partly because of the very *real* conspiracies I've written about in such books as *Chameleo* and *Cryptoscatology*. He continues to appeal to this anti-government mentality, but as always his words amount to nothing more than hollow platitudes. It should be obvious to anyone that his policies were never "anti-government." As recently as December of 2018, Trump hinted that the Pentagon's budget needed to be severely limited,[92] but when it came time to announce that budget he ended up giving the Pentagon five percent *more* money than they had requested in the first place.[93]

Trump's presence in the White House served as the perfect distraction from the forces that are actually killing us. He's a giant, blustering voodoo doll of a puppet that barfs out hatred and fear on command, a hypnotic green goo so vulgar—and so captivating as a result—that it occupied the fickle and unsophisticated attention of the masses while their fellow Americans remain trapped in prisons made of unseen bars . . . all right in front of the blank-eyed faces, the rage-fueled minds of the citizenry, conned like marks on a street corner staring in wonder and anger as the Idiot-Savant-Magician in front of them pulled off the greatest and most simplistic illusions in history with little more than misspelled tweets and sensationalistic bon mots specifically constructed to bypass one's capacity to *think*.

As the opposition wasted their time attempting to combat every single stupid one-liner that emerged from the White House, the most horrendous criminals of all continued to slip right on by. In sight of cameras. In sight of reporters. In sight of everyone. Invisible, but only to those who refused to *see*.

Operation Mindfuck has been a tremendous success. It resulted in four years of Trump, the religious hijacking of the Supreme Court, the brainwashing of thousands of Americans via a live-action roleplaying game called "QAnon" (the effects of which can still be felt today), and the erosion of the left wing in America thanks to a constant barrage of strategic distractions.

Far more useful than dreaming about removing the President from office through impeachment would have been a genuine effort to reverse the laws that have made this "new approach to slavery" possible in the first place. Back in 1994, in the last chapter of his revised edition of *Operation Mind Control*, my friend and colleague Walter Bowart wrote:

> Whatever the motive for the creation of the National Security State, it was the beginning of the end of our free society [. . .]. The Bill of Rights says freedom of speech is one of our inalienable rights. But as an ordinary citizen living in the National Security State you don't *know* anything truly relevant to talk about. If you're being kept in the informational dark, you can't talk about the future. Keeping you secretly in the dark about vital information impairs your thinking. And if your thinking is impaired, your speaking is impaired. That means your freedom of speech *is* impaired.
>
> Remember Thomas Jefferson's remark at the beginning of this book: " . . . there is no safe depository of the ultimate powers of society but the people themselves, and if we think them not enlightened enough to exercise their control with a wholesome discretion, the remedy is not to take it from them, but to inform their discretion by education." The practices of a national security state preclude that. The control has been taken from us. The democratic processes of government

today must be just for show—a feeble attempt to keep the public order.

That's when a simple thought began to form in my mind. My parents' generation wanted to drink without sneaking around so they repealed the Volstead Act which prohibited the consumption of alcohol. It ought to be easy. This generation ought to be wise enough to repeal the National Security Act which prohibits freedom of information, therefore freedom of thought—and therefore freedom of speech. Since the founding fathers never anticipated the invention of technologies that would intrude themselves into a person's private thoughts, even take over and drive his dreams, should we consider adding another amendment to the Constitution which guarantees freedom of thought? One would like to believe that, once the legal debate concluded and all the testimony about the role of language (speech) in thought processes had been established, the Supreme Court would agree that the right of free speech was based upon the presumption of free thought. But there needs to be debate about it now, so that the invisible and uninvited deliberate influences upon the human mind will be mandated illegal by the courts [. . .].

It's up to us to read the books on the National Security Act. Learn the lingo, then, armed with the facts, start calling for the repeal of it. At this time it would appear to be unthinkable. The National Security State would appear to be a given, something taken for granted like the air we breathe. But try telling people you're working to repeal it and watch them want to join you [. . .].

We can all at once repeal the National Security Act, and all the secret agencies under it which violate our Constitutional rights. Why tell the truth one declassified document at a time, or thirty-three million declassified documents at a time? Why not do it all at once by abolishing the National Security Act?

The National Security Act has taken the truth away. We are, in fact, living in a state of Martial Law, a state of National Emergency. They call it national security. Where's the security in it? Without freedom, without civil rights, what kind of security can a people have?[94]

When Bowart wrote those words, he couldn't have known that we were only seven years away from the devastating effects of 9/11 and the passing of the Patriot Act. He couldn't have known that he was only thirteen years away from his own death (Bowart passed away from colon cancer on December 18, 2007). Nonetheless, even knowing the Phantom Carriage would be coming for him, I don't think he would have altered his challenging, provocative words in any way. If he were alive today, Bowart would no doubt be adamant about the repeal of the Patriot Act, something that should have occurred during the eight years of Barack Obama's presidency (but, of course, never did). Because the true power lies not in the White House, but in the will of the people to influence those who inhabit the White House.

The repeal of the National Security Act and the Patriot Act can and will happen . . . *if* the people wake up from their collective dream and realize what's really important, where the real fight lies. Abolishing the National Security Act and the Patriot Act should be the first goals on the agenda of any progressive who wishes to make a real difference in how the United States operates on a day-to-day basis. Once you unlock the door to the National Security State, you also unlock the door to the future. As Bowart says, it's impossible to engage in genuine freedom of thought if all the most cutting-edge discoveries and advancements have been systemically withheld from the common person. Outside the hermetically sealed, solipsistic universe of the military-industrial-entertainment-complex, the common person is always a generation or more behind the times.

There's still time to reclaim Operation Mindfuck. We reclaim it by shunting it aside. Who needs tricks and pranks anymore? We need to take advantage of laws that already exist to rip the tattered and yellowed National Security Blanket from the cold, arthritic, militaristic fists of those in power. Then we boot the poor bastards (and I'm not just talking about Trump and his cronies) out into the cold, with all the other obsolete spies and politicians and persuasion engineers, and let them fend for themselves in this "shithole country."

Don't allow yourself to be hypnotized by the green goo.

Simply keep your eyes focused on the dirty secret sitting out in the open on a mantelpiece constructed by Edgar Allan Poe 178 years ago.

★

"The autumn months are never a calm time in America. Back to Work, Back to Football Practice, etc. . . . Autumn is a very Traditional period, a time of strong Rituals and the celebrating of strange annual holidays like Halloween and Satanism and the fateful Harvest Moon, which can have ominous implications for some people.

"Autumn is always a time of Fear and Greed and Hoarding for the winter coming on. Debt collectors are active on old people and fleece the weak and helpless. They want to lay in enough cash to weather the known horrors of January and February. There is always a rash of kidnapping and abductions of schoolchildren in the football months. Preteens of both sexes are traditionally seized and grabbed off the streets by gangs of organized perverts who traditionally give them as Christmas gifts to each other to be personal sex slaves and playthings.

"Most of these things are obviously Wrong and Evil and Ugly—but at least they are Traditional. They will happen. Your driveway will ice over, your furnace will blow up, and you will be rammed in traffic by an uninsured driver in a stolen car.

"But what the hell? That's why we have Insurance, eh? And the Inevitability of these nightmares is what makes them so reassuring. Life will go on, for good or ill. But some things are forever, right? The structure may be a little Crooked, but the foundations are still strong and unshakable.

"Ho ho. Think again, buster. Look around you. There is an eerie sense of Panic in the air, a silent Fear and uncertainty that comes with once-reliable faiths and truths and solid Institutions that are no longer safe to believe in. . . . There is a Presidential Election, right on schedule, but somehow there is no President. A new Congress is elected, like always, but somehow there is no real Congress at all—not as we knew it, anyway, and whatever passes for Congress will be as helpless and weak as whoever has to pass for the 'New President.'"

—Hunter S. Thompson, *Hey Rube: Blood Sport, the Bush Doctrine, and the Downward Spiral of Dumbness*, 2004

PART THREE

IF YOU'RE INTO EATING
CHILDREN'S BRAINS,
YOU'VE GOT A FOUR-
YEAR FREE RIDE:
A QANON BEDTIME STORY

"Well, who ya gonna believe? Me or your own eyes?"

—Chico Marx, *Duck Soup*, 1933

I'm writing this on Saturday, November 7, 2020, the day Joe Biden was declared the forty-sixth president of the United States. On my television, thousands of Biden's supporters are cheering and dancing in the streets of Los Angeles, shouting transcendental cries of relief out of open second-floor windows.

Not everyone in the country is reacting with such joy. Of course, this would be true of any presidential election. Nothing unusual there. But 2020 is not a usual year in numerous ways. 2020 is a year in which thousands of citizens absolutely refuse to recognize reality when they see it. They call themselves "red-pilled," drawing upon the terminology of the Wachowskis' *The Matrix*. In QAnon-speak, to "red-pill" is to accept as unassailable truth the conspiracy theory that elitist occultists are ruling the world from behind the scenes by eating the brains of children and that Donald Trump is the only man who can save us from this evil cabal, while to "blue-pill" is to align yourself with the Democratic Party and become mere "sheeple" who believe only what mainstream news-casters and scientists *tell* you is true. Yes, that's right: despite being fearful of an imagined dark world in which Celine Dion is lacing her children's clothing line with a chemical that makes children "gender neutral" as part of a vast satanic scheme,[95] these "Christian Patriots" have embraced—as the central metaphor of their new religion—a science-fictional concept created over twenty years ago by *two transgender women*. "Cognitive Dissonance" doesn't even begin to describe the confused state of mind with which these people must wrestle on a daily basis.

In my five-part *Salon* series about the little-known origins of QAnon, I wrote about the loopiness of a "Christian Patriot" radio show called *The B2T Show*. During the first episode that aired after the 2020 presidential election, a Christian seer calling herself "Amanda Grace" revealed what the Lord God Yahweh told her about Donald Trump's 2020 landslide victory. (You heard right: Trump's "landslide victory.") The venerable hosts of the show, Rick and his weird friend Gene, helped Amanda explain to their viewers that wicked "destroyers" disguised as postal workers thwarted Trump's reelection by tainting, shredding, and switching vital pieces of pro-Trump ballots. Their proof? Why, the voice of God appeared in Amanda's skull at 3:00 A.M. and told her all of this, of course. What else?

★

"Now, the Lord usually repeats himself before something's about to happen. I've noticed this."

—Amanda Grace, The B2T Show, 11-4-20

★

Rick & Gene insisted that Trump's "white hats" (the mythical angels that are helping Trump from behind the scenes even though, for some reason, they failed to help the Great Man get reelected) have cleverly set up the Democrats with a "blockchain watermark system" on every ballot. As a result, Biden and his cohorts will be arrested lickety-split. At one point in the episode, Rick even insists—with a straight face—that without voter fraud, the electoral map would have been completely red. In the upper left corner of Rick's personal map, one can see Biden's face with a "zero" right next to it. These "Christian Patriots" seriously believe that Biden received zero legitimate votes in 2020. Zero.[96]

★

"Nothing is so painful to the human mind as a great and sudden change."

—Mary Shelley, *Frankenstein*, 1818

★

On November 6, 2020, *The Washington Post* reported the arrests of two QAnon acolytes near the Philadelphia convention center where votes from the presidential election were still being counted:

Philadelphia police said they located the armed men [Joshua Macias and Antonio LaMotta] near the convention center late Thursday after being tipped off about people with guns traveling there in a silver Hummer with Virginia license plates. Police found the Hummer and then two bike patrol officers spotted the two men, both of whom were arrested for having guns they were not allowed to carry in the city [. . .].

Photos of the Hummer captured what appeared to be a hat inside bearing an insignia for QAnon, a far-right conspiracy theory, as well as a decal on its rear window bearing an abbreviation of that group's rallying cry, "Where we go one, we go all."

In a statement announcing the charges Friday, [Philadelphia District Attorney Larry] Krasner said police had been told the armed people were coming to Philadelphia, "possibly for a reason related to the ongoing canvas of votes." He also said the investigation is ongoing and that more charges could follow.

Danielle Outlaw, the Philadelphia police commissioner, said LaMotta was seen carrying a 9mm pistol visible in a hip holster, while Macias had a handgun concealed under his jacket. Outlaw said that Macias had a Virginia concealed carry permit. After the men gave police consent to search their Hummer, an AR-15-style rifle was recovered inside it, she said. In total, Krasner said about 160 rounds of ammunition were found.[97]

The next day, on November 7, *The Times of India* reported:

> Two heavily armed men "coming to deliver a truck full of fake ballots" have been arrested near the Philadelphia convention center where election workers were counting votes from the undecided US presidential election, police said. Antonio LaMotta, 61, and Joshua Macias, 42, both of Chesapeake, Virginia, were arrested on Thursday night outside the center on suspicion of carrying handguns in Pennsylvania state without permits, according to US media reports [. . .].
>
> Details about the alleged fake ballots—including where they came from, whether they were found in the Hummer, or what was marked on them—were not immediately available, CNN reported.
>
> It's unclear what those men were allegedly intending to do. The FBI and Philadelphia Police are investigating the incident, CBS News reported.
>
> Prosecutors say text messages show the men say they were concerned about the vote counting happening at the Convention Center and they were "coming to deliver a truck full of fake ballots to Philly." [. . .]
>
> Stickers and a hat with logos of the far-right QAnon conspiracy movement were found in the vehicle, Philadelphia District Attorney Larry Krasner said. . . .[98]

In June of 2020, a QAnon follower named Alpalus Slyman kidnapped his own children (five of them) in order to prevent them from being kidnapped by the Deep State. Even while being chased by a swarm of cops down a highway in Massachusetts,

Slyman had the presence of mind to livestream the daring "rescue." He yelled into the camera, "Donald Trump, I need a miracle or something! QAnon, help me! QAnon, help me!"

Here's an excerpt from Will Sommer's August 16, 2020 *Daily Beast* article about the incident:

> Inspired by [QAnon] videos he had watched online, Slyman warned his children during the chase that the police were coming to abduct them—or maybe just shoot them in a staged killing. In return, they begged him to pull over. His daughter even tried to grab the wheel of the minivan and drive it off the road after he accused her and his wife, who had dived out of the vehicle at the start of the chase, of being agents of the nefarious cabal that QAnon believers say controls the world.
>
> "They want to make us crazy," Slyman said, "but I'm not crazy. My wife and my daughter were a part of it."
>
> Desperate, Slyman's daughter told her father she was working for the mythical cabal in a failed attempt to scare him into stopping the minivan. Then Slyman told his children, who ranged from 8 months to 13 years old, about the QAnon belief that a video of Hillary Clinton and aide Huma Abedin eating childrens' brains was discovered on Anthony Weiner's laptop.
>
> Days earlier, Slyman had watched a video pushing exactly that claim on a YouTube channel operated by Timothy Charles Holmseth, a QAnon promoter who claims to work for a secretive government agency called the Pentagon Pedophile Task Force.
>
> There is no Pentagon Pedophile Task Force. But there in the middle of a high-speed chase, Slyman spouted that baseless claim to his children anyway.
>
> "Hillary's demonic," Slyman said. "I know about Hillary cutting open a 10-year-old. And Huma Abedin."

> New Hampshire police blew out Slyman's tires, but he
> kept going. The chase only ended when Slyman crashed into
> a police cruiser, then drove his minivan into a tree.[99]

An unending loop of your basest fears funneled back into your
basal ganglia through strategically composed lies can only lead
to a funhouse-mirror view of life, particularly when the brain
in question is already disordered to begin with. Even the most
extreme fanatic can fight reality for only so long. Sooner or
later, you have one of two choices to make: 1) Either wake up
and acknowledge that you allowed yourself to be conned into
accepting pure illusion as truth or 2) Embrace the illusion fully
and live inside it 24/7. Mr. Alpalus Slyman chose the latter path.
He "blue-pilled" while incessantly and maniacally claiming he
had done the exact opposite.

Despite what "Amanda Grace" was told by the Lord God
Yahweh, the only verifiable reports of criminals being arrested
with "fake ballots" in their possession were a pair of QAnon
followers.

Despite what Alpalus Slyman was told by the Lord God
QAnon, the only verifiable reports of criminals being arrested
with kidnapped children in their possession while ranting and
raving about "eating childrens' brains" was a QAnon follower
named Alpalus Slyman.

To better comprehend the shape and shadow of this new
American religion, I decided to sign up for the *B2T Show* news-
letter using a Gmail address associated with a skillfully crafted
pseudonym through which not even the most steely-eyed, astute,
Sherlock-Holmesian observer could penetrate: "Edgar Allan
Poe." I know what you're thinking: Did Mr. Poe know I was
appropriating his identity? Yes, of course. Naturally, I received
his permission before embarking on this delicate psyop.

Poe's email address is edapoe09@gmail.com (in case you don't know, Mr. Poe was born in 1809). In March of 2020, just after the lockdown, Mr. Poe guest-blogged for my *Cryptoscatology* website, contributing an Op-Ed piece entitled "The Masque of the Red Death."[100] When I invited him to guest-blog for me, I was hoping he would help my readers get their minds *off* the pandemic, but that's not what happened. (Poe's not exactly a happy camper.)

Seconds after submitting Poe's email address to the *B2T Show* website, I received the following boilerplate response:

Hey Ed,

I've never been the most political guy. I didn't have the time for it (or so I thought).

I work full time for a large tech consulting company. [For some reason, Rick does not wish to advertise the fact that he works for IBM. Is it because he's constantly railing against the satanic evils of "Big Tech"?]

I'm a dad and a Christian and love the Bible. I used to fill my time teaching Bible classes at my church and coaching my kids in sports or watching/paying [sic] sports.

It was 2015 when the seeds of my "take the blue pill or the red pill" moment were planted.

My son, who was 17 at the time, sent me a YouTube video link and asked me to check it out.

Having no idea what I was getting myself into, I watched the video he sent me.

And I admit, it seemed pretty out there. Definitely stuff you don't hear from the Mainstream Media or the News Apps on my phone where I was getting my news at the time.

"Is my kid a conspiracy theorist?" I remember wondering. . . especially as he continued sending me more and more videos, many discussing topics that were weird or just seemed impossible.

And I was turned way off by some of the abrasive personalities delivering the information, with some even yelling and screaming at the camera.

But, to connect with my son—and keep a watchful eye—I kept watching these and other videos he'd sent me.

The more I listened, the more I was able to see past the presentation styles, and LISTEN to what they were actually saying.

I became intrigued enough to research these "crazy theories."

And much to MY shock, there was a lot more truth behind them than I'd have ever believed.

As I kept digging, I kept finding valleys as wide and deep as the Grand Canyon between what the mainstream media reported and what was actually truthful.

Like I said, Trump getting nominated shocked the heck out of me. I hadn't voted for him in the primary but now I started seeing through the hateful media coverage on Trump.

By now I'd taken "the red pill," and not only was there no turning back, I knew I couldn't keep my findings to myself.

My first attempt to share them, publicly, was pretty disappointing.

We've all got to start someplace, though, even if we fall on our face, right?

Donald Trump "fell on his face" in his past as he nearly went bankrupt several times, but he persisted against giant odds and became successful. When running for President, the establishment underestimated him, and they were the ones who were most shocked when he won the nomination.

Were you surprised when Trump won the nomination to run on the Republican ticket? Excited? Was it an answer to prayer? Were you shocked like I was when Donald Trump won?

Or did you believe from the start?

Hit reply and let me know. I'd love to hear.

Talk soon,

Rick B2T

So this Christian tech guy, who used to spend most of his time "watching/paying [sic] sports," receives a few links to some raucous Alex Jones videos from his disaffected teenage progeny and takes a deep dive into madness. Over the next couple of years, in the wake of QAnon's appearance in October of 2017, this leads to a YouTube channel that boasted more than ninety thousand subscribers before it was taken down just a few weeks before the election in a sudden move on YouTube's part to crack down on "conspiracy theory content used to justify real-world violence."[101]

I can see it now: Rick B2T goes out of his way to create this YouTube empire built on rightwing conspiracy theories just to impress his son. He turns to his kid one afternoon and says, "Hey, you've gotta admit . . . Pops is pretty cool, right?" And his son says, through heavy-lidded, bloodshot, stoned eyes, "Huh? Oh . . . *whut?* Conspiracy theories? Aw . . . leave me alone, man. I'm not into that crap any more, Dad. I've moved on to veganism, Buddhism, and autoerotic strangulation. Let me send you a few links about all that stuff instead . . ." Well, Rick can't base a YouTube channel on *those subjects,* not if he wants to remain in the same church to which he's been tithing for the past two decades, so he just powers on with the QAnon propaganda even though—in some deep, cellular part of his brain—he *must* know by now that it's complete bullshit.

But you wouldn't know that by listening to his nightly pronouncements.

★

It's now November 9 and Rick B2T is telling his followers that Pennsylvania is no longer projecting Biden as the winner; the entire state has been returned to the undecided category on the electoral map. No reliable source is reporting this. "Ignore the fake news!" he says several times in between advertisements urging his loyal viewers to invest in gold. He's also insisting that the Fox News broadcasters are far too leftwing for his tastes, nothing more than "controlled opposition" who are secretly working for the Deep State. He urges his viewers to abandon Fox News for Newsmax, Christopher Ruddy's ultra-conservative streaming service. Any source reporting that Trump is *not* the real winner of the 2020 election is tipping their hand, revealing the irrefutable fact that they're in cahoots with the Deep State.[102]

Rick lays out how he believes "the Cabal" rigged the election for Biden:

"Remember: We were winning Wisconsin, we were winning Michigan, as well as Georgia, as well as Pennsylvania, when we all went to bed. And they closed down the voting machines to try to figure out how many votes they needed. And because of the awesome job *you* all did, getting out there and voting—the in-person vote won every state except for New York. And it was so overwhelming, it overwhelmed the cheating they had planned on, such as the algorithms taking three percent of the vote away from the counties with what they call the Dominion Software. A lot more is going to be coming out about the Dominion Software. And you'll see that that [software] was *flipping*. We've seen two examples of it now, where we literally see the exact number of votes going out of a Republican and into a Democrat. There was one that literally showed that. It went from Trump to Biden, the exact number of votes for that minute. So it was 560 votes the first time, and it was a significant amount of votes that moved to Joe Biden. I think it was 19,000 or so. *Huge* numbers! But in-person voting overwhelmed their cheating, so they had to go back to manual cheating. And that's where they're gonna get *nailed!*"[103]

The definitive book about the history of voter fraud in the United States is *Votescam: The Stealing of America* by James and Kenneth Collier. A significant portion of the Collier Brothers' book deals with massive corruption in Dade County, Florida. I found a paperback copy of *Votescam* in 1994 at Either/Or, a sorely missed bookstore once located right across from the Hermosa Beach pier. Imagine my surprise when, in 2000, the entire election pivoted on accusations of fraud in none other than . . . Dade County, Florida. I felt as if I had been privileged enough to stumble across some sort of mystical screenplay laying out weirdly specific future events.

In December of 2000, *Salon* published Greg Palast's in-depth analysis of voter fraud in the 2000 elections entitled "Florida's Flawed 'Voter-cleansing' Program." Palast's analysis centered on a particular geographical location, which would be far easier to rig than an entire country.[104] The reason I find Palast's coverage of the 2000 election far more compelling than the accusations I've heard regarding the 2020 election is that I don't hear a lot of *specific examples* of voter fraud being cited. What I'm hearing essentially amounts to rumors or secondhand accounts. Where's the evidence Rick claims to have in his possession? He says he has "two examples," but doesn't back up the claim with anything concrete (and Rick's going to need a lot more than just two examples to convince anyone of these accusations). At the moment, these are just blustering pronouncements that seem akin to wish fulfillment.

Another question I have is this: If "the Cabal" had the capability to pull this off in 2020, why didn't they rig the election for Hillary in 2016?

Perhaps this leads us in a different and far more disturbing direction. Let's say QAnon is correct, that this occult "cabal" has been in charge of the entire American shebang for the past several decades. When did *their* control begin? With Bill Clinton in 1992? Or were George H. W. Bush and Ronald Reagan also pawns on the Illuminati chessboard? If so, why wouldn't this same "cabal" have total control of the 2016 election, just like they did with every election that preceded it? Therefore, can we not conclude that Trump was *their* chosen candidate in 2016?

Hey, I'm sorry, Rick, am I asking too many questions? Perhaps I should just shut my trap and "Trust the Plan."

★

"There's nothing [Trump] tweets that doesn't come true. Right? Just think back all the way when they attacked Trump for tweeting lies when he said he was being wiretapped. And he was, right? So almost everything he says—I don't know if he has a looking-glass or if he's just got a mass of information from military intel. I personally believe he has *both*, but everything he says is correct."

—Rick Rene, *The B2T Show*, 11-9-20

★

It's now November 11 and Rick is telling his followers that only *nineteen* states voted for Biden (despite the fact that two days earlier he insisted that *no* states voted for Biden). He then directs his loyal viewers to a website called EveryLegalVote.com where one can view an electoral map of the United States through the lens of two dramatically different buttons. When you click on the left button (marked "With Voter Fraud"), the map shows 306 electoral votes for Biden and 232 for Trump. When you click the right button (marked "Without Voter Fraud"), the map shows 220 electoral votes for Biden and 318 for Trump.

You see? You clicked the button, the screen changed, and unadorned reality was unveiled before your eyes. And this mystical illumination came about without psilocybin, ayahuasca, or Adrenochrome extracted from pre-legal pineal glands. It's difficult to argue with the absolute truth when it's laid out for you so conveniently, right there on your glowing screen. It's rather like a magical looking glass, isn't it? Like looking through a beautifully crafted stained-glass window, right into the heart of Reality Itself. Like a fairy tale come true.

Later in this same episode, Rick stares into his camera and revels in giving his audience the Good News: "President Trump is currently winning the 2020 election with most states won, and he holds the lead in the Electoral voting. The President now holds 232 Electoral College votes to Biden's 226. The President has won twenty-five states to Biden's nineteen. There are six states still in question. You'll never get this fair reporting from the corrupt news. They are trying to anoint [Biden]. They create fear, and they're trying to feed on that fear and change timelines. They're trying to change the future timeline to what we all start thinking. If we start *thinking* in fear, and *thinking* like this, and let all the media do the work for us . . . that's why, turn off that TV! Turn off Fox News! Turn on Newsmax, if you're going to have the TV on, or otherwise go to programs like this. Go to Bitchute—to your other favorite QTubers, if you will, and I think you'll really enjoy staying *out* of the Fake News media for a while."

In this most challenging time marked by flux and chaos, Rick is advising his flock to seal themselves off from any point of view that differs from the reality in which they wish to live rather than the one that exists. Is this the best method for survival in a time of crisis?

Welcome to the Disassociated States of America.

★

After the election, Q went dark for over a week. If you listened closely, you could hear the grating sound of thousands of Q-heads biting their nails throughout this prolonged silence from Trump's most important covert intelligence advisor. The last post before Biden's victory read as follows:

> **that this nation, under God, shall have a new birth of freedom and that government of the people, by the people, for the people, shall not perish from the earth.**
> **- Abraham Lincoln Nov 1863 Together we win.**[105]

This was accompanied by a YouTube link to the soundtrack of Michael Mann's *The Last of the Mohicans* (1992).

Upon seeing this "drop," I immediately thought: *This* is the most inspiring message they can come up with one day before the election?

It was almost as if the various members of Team QAnon were bored silly with the assignment and couldn't wait for it to end.

★

"We've had about eight days of darkness, if you will. 11-3 was the last [Q] drop [. . .]. Hopefully, we'll get some [new Q drops] on Friday. That would be ten days, if he's doing the ten-day thing. But I never expect that. You know . . . he's gone longer than ten days. Sometimes twenty-one days. Who knows? The point is, he's got us thinking for *ourselves*. That is the point of this whole thing."

—Rick Rene, *The B2T Show*, 11-11-20

★

At last, on November 12, Team QAnon pops their head out of the sand with an uncharacteristically gentle assurance that borders on the motherly in tone:

It had to be this way.

Sometimes you must walk through the darkness before you see the light.[106]

This Hallmark card can't possibly assuage the seething hordes who have been waiting to see Biden's severed head hanging from a lamppost in Washington, D.C.

After reading the above "Q drop" to his audience at the beginning of his November 13 (Friday the 13th) podcast, Rick attempts to calm his virtual parishioners: "There are a lot of people who feel apprehension right now. I'm asking you to *please* keep that faith. Do not be anxious about anything. In every situation (and this is one of those situations, right?), by prayer and petition, with thanksgiving, present your request to God. And if you do that, He promises what? The peace of God that transcends *all* understanding. The peace of God that transcends *all* understanding will guard your hearts and minds in Christ Jesus! That peace that transcends *all* understanding! And that's why Q says, 'It had to be this way.' We're gettin' those three birds with *one* stone. The criminal, cheating Democrats, *boom*! Criminal Big Tech, *poosh*! Criminal media. Over the next couple of months, they're all going to be completely exposed, right?

And so there might be some rough times, but, heck . . . sometimes you must walk through the darkness before you see the light."[107]

I don't know how long Rick's assurances are going to keep this QAnon crowd pacified. And neither does Rick.

Mere days before the election, Q posted a barrage of adrenaline-pumping questions like a football coach intent on ramping up his players' enthusiasm before the most important game of the century:

> *Are you ready to finish what we started?*[108]
> *Are you ready to hold the political elite accountable?*[109]
> *Are you ready to take back control of this Country?*[110]

A sad, defeatist post like **"It had to be this way"** seems rather anticlimactic by comparison. Where the hell did all the bravado go?

Despite Rick's hollow assurances, a lot of Trump's acolytes are growing more and more freaked out by Q's failure to bring about the "Great Awakening" that he/she/they have been promising for so many years. Some of them are already beginning to retcon the entire QAnon phenomenon in order to maintain the peculiar worldview that Q helped instill in them in the first place. Aubrey Huff, a former Major League Baseball player (for the San Francisco Giants and the Detroit Tigers, among others), sent out the following tweet on Saturday, November 4:

Aubrey Huff
@aubrey_huff
· 4h
Qanon was a democratic strategy to keep many conservatives complacent in "trusting the plan" while the left continued their evil corruption.

In Aubrey Huff's mind, Q's overarching conspiratorial worldview is still firmly in place—and, in keeping with the QAnon phenomenon, wrongdoings committed by the right are flipped and blamed on the left. Perhaps this marks the future of QAnon: QAnon without QAnon. Just drop the label and rebrand. Maybe some other anonymous poster will soon pop up offering salvation through hatred, paranoia, racism, xenophobia, neophobia, and plain, good old-fashioned, All-American *fear.*

Who knows?

Maybe it'll even be *you.*

★

It's now November 15 and the atmosphere's feeling rather desperate in Rick's DIY home studio. After shilling his new line of "Christian Patriot" sanitizers (do these products sanitize non-Christian, unpatriotic germs?), Rick attempts to sell his audience the following castle in the sky: "This is a movie we're watching and we're going to be envisioning Trump as the victor . . . because I just want to see that happen anyway, no matter which way this goes in this military-intelligence operation . . . as they make more mistakes and try to lie to us some more. It's *not* going to work!"

Is even Rick beginning to vacillate? A few days earlier, Rick told us Trump would remain in the White House without question. But now he's throwing in qualifiers like "no matter which way this goes." Did God change his omniscient mind at some point between Amanda Grace's November 4th appearance on the show and now? What could possibly put a crick in God's plan to continue Trump's administration? Is reality itself opposed to God's divine blueprint?

Later in the show, certain aspects of Rick's personality are revealed. As he reads from a Q-head's blog to prove that Biden and his cohorts will soon be tossed into prison for election rigging, he decides to share his computer screen with the audience. The post from which he's reading is visible for all to see. The post begins with this line: **"How come you faggots aren't reporting THIS???"** This is followed by a link to yet more unprovable jabberwocky. Rick reads aloud the entire post *except for that first sentence.* The sentence lingers on his screen for a very long time. Rick can clearly see it. It doesn't make him bat an eye or even wince in embarrassment.[111] Is the word "faggot" used so commonly around Rick's wholesome Texan household that it doesn't even occur to him to try to explain it away or to switch to another screen as quickly as possible?

Throughout the episode, from time to time, the following invitation appears above Rick's head, with a hyperlink: DISCUSS Q WITH B2T & OTHER ANONS.

So I accept. Who can resist such genteel Southern hospitality? I follow the link to a site called Voat.

The *very first message* I see is a vehement and (not surprisingly) anonymous screed about the poster's desperate need to chase down "niggers."

I decide that investigating the site any further is not necessary.

Ten days later, on Christmas Day, I discover that Voat—which had been around for six years—is now disabled. In its place is a link to a message written by the site's creator explaining that Voat has run out of funds. The explanation ends with two quotes from the Bible:

Dearly beloved, avenge not yourselves, but rather give place unto wrath: for it is written, "Vengeance is mine; I will repay", saith the Lord. Romans 12:19

&

Do not say, "I will do to him as he has done to me; I will pay the man back for what he has done." Proverbs 24:29[112]

The very first comment one sees after this heartfelt farewell is: "Goodbye and Merry Christmas niggerfaggot" followed by "Thank you Patriot!" and "Thank you for the best site, EVER, truly remarkable. Love you guys. No mercy, no quarter. JESUS IS KING!"

. . . followed by 2,455 comments in a similar vein: breathless paeans to Jesus alternating with racist, homophobic screeds.

One can only wonder why Christians get such a bad rap these days.

★

It's now November 21, and I'm standing in line with my wife at a Sears in Long Beach. My wife is returning some pants she'd purchased for our daughter a few days before. The pants were too small. A woman at the front of the long line is taking an inordinate amount of time returning what appears to be a defective metal kitchen appliance. Suffering from near-terminal boredom, I glance up at the ceiling and notice a green Christmas wreath dangling above me. It occurs to me that if one added a tiny tail at the bottom, the wreath would look like the letter "Q."

I turn to my wife and say, "Hey . . . we should make some cheap QAnon Christmas wreaths and sell them at overinflated prices to these brainwashed fucks."

"That's a really good idea," my wife says.

The second I get home, I google "QAnon Christmas wreath." The only match is a ceramic QAnon ornament that depicts a white rabbit leaping over the letter Q. (The white rabbit is a recurring symbol in QAnon mythology. One would think the rabbit was derived from *Alice in Wonderland*, but instead most of the Q-heads seem to associate the rabbit only with *The Matrix*; they don't appear to be aware that the Wachowskis' use of the rabbit was an overt reference to the writings of Lewis Carroll.) Amazon describes this ornament as a "Trust in the Plan" gift that's ideal for Christmas, weddings, and birthdays. Its theme is identified as "religious" in nature. This holy trinket will only set you back $12.99, plus $6.99 shipping and handling.

The total lack of QAnon-themed Christmas wreaths shocks me. Clearly, this is a void that needs to be filled by some enterprising entrepreneur. Search for me on Etsy under the name "Pelosi'sPittsburghPlatterPingPongPizzaParlor" or perhaps "BidenHarrisClevelandSteamer." I haven't decided yet.

★

It's now November 22, the fifty-seventh anniversary of the JFK assassination, and Gene is on Rick's show pumping up the faithful with the lowdown on the Deep State conspiracy arrayed against Trump's second term.

Gene: "[Trump] got 80% of *every* state! What this did is, it overwhelmed the algorithm of the Dominion machine and its software. It wasn't capable of dealing with that, so they had to shut it down and reboot it and bring in tons of fake ballots and all kind of things. Because [Trump] swept the country! The Republicans swept the country! And so once all this comes to light, there's going to be a lot of people going to Gitmo or Camp Century or various other FEMA camps they [the Illuminati] designed for *us* [Christians] . . . "

Rick: "Now, Gene, this is a gut feeling. There's no evidence I have, but I just feel there's already military tribunals going on for the voter fraud right now that are secret, just like there has been for the last three years."

Gene: "Two days ago twelve big transport planes left for Gitmo."

Rick: "Wow!"

Gene: "So I do know *that* occurred."

Rick: "That's some potential evidence there, right? Whether it's back to the whole Spygate or the human trafficking and everything else going on, or it's this voter fraud, we know there's always been stuff going on behind the scenes with the white hats in control. And that's why the media and the entire apparatus of the Deep State is trying to get us to think and change time-lines to this negative timeline that Joe Biden is actually going to become President on January 20th when we know for a *fact* that Donald J. Trump is going to be President on January 20th! That's why we need to be faith-praying with the vision of that happening. Correct, Gene?"

Gene: "It's like I said last night. You either have faith or you *don't*. If you have disbelief, you're serving Satan."[113]

★

When one listens to Rick and his friends over an extended period of time, one begins to realize that they truly believe they can alter reality—"timelines," as they like to say—merely by thinking about the desired results long and hard enough. Not by prayer, per se, but through actual *magic*. They believe they're countering the sigil-wielding Satanists in Hollywood with the enemy's own occult weapons.

You might call them magic-practicing "Christian Patriots," which on the surface would seem to be a contradiction in terms, but they see no conflict of interest in Christians practicing magic in God's name. In this sense they're mimicking the way their hero, Donald Trump, was raised.

Not long after Election Day, media theorist Douglas Rushkoff (the aforementioned author of *Program or Be Programmed* and many other books) visits writer and practicing magician Grant Morrison in Scotland to discuss Morrison's views on magic and creativity in relation to current events. The interview airs on Rushkoff's podcast, *Team Human*. During their conversation, Morrison touches on this seeming paradox of the far-right-wing appropriating the tools of magic for their own ends:

> Morrison: As the Left became more divided and more turned against itself, I think the Right took up the ideas of magic to the point where the President lives in a world of magical thinking. "If I deny this, it will cease to be. My will is stronger than reality." He genuinely exists in that bubble where he truly believes that by thinking it hard enough, by repeating it again and again, it *will* become reality.
>
> Rushkoff: And there's some truth to that, there's some logic. I mean, it's the way magic works. [Trump] was raised in the Church of Norman Vincent Peale, the guy who wrote *The Power of Positive Thinking*.
>
> Morrison: The power of positive thinking to overturn tornadoes, to turn back tides and fires. I think [Trump] truly has that in him. Clearly, the magic has worked, and it's worked in a lot of interesting ways, but it's maybe time for some of the people on what used to be "our side" to reclaim it. There's such a polarization right now that maybe everyone kind of has to meet in the middle again using the same [magical] techniques.

Rushkoff: You know, I always wanted to believe that bad people couldn't use magic, that you had to have some sort of integrity and connection to Godhead.

Morrison: [Laughs] But we've all seen those movies [with] the black magician—Baron Mordo from *Doctor Strange*. We should've known, we should've understood, that *they're* equally good at it.[114]

This is the main reason Rick encourages his audience to avoid watching mainstream news. It's not to shield them from the pain of a fallen world. He believes that if enough "Christian Patriots" divest themselves of consensus reality, reality *itself* will change. So when Rick makes statements that aren't true, he's not lying— not from his perspective. He's just practicing magic. Fighting occult fire with occult fire.

But what happens when the magic fails?

What happens when reality simply refuses to change at your bidding?

★

On December 6, Sanjana Karanth of *The Huffington Post* reports the following:

> Supporters of President Donald Trump amped up their efforts to intimidate Michigan officials this weekend, gathering with firearms outside Secretary of State Jocelyn Benson's home on Saturday to protest the battleground state's election results, which helped Joe Biden win the race.
>
> Benson, who is Michigan's top election official, released a statement on Sunday speaking out about the incident. She said that dozens of armed individuals stood outside her home "shouting obscenities and chanting into bullhorns" while she

was decorating the house for Christmas with her 4-year-old son.

"The demands made outside my home were unambiguous, loud and threatening. They targeted me in my role as Michigan's Chief Election Officer," Benson said. "But the threats of those gathered weren't actually aimed at me — or any other elected officials in this state. They were aimed at the voters."[115]

A little over a week later, on the 14th, Chris Matthews of *MarketWatch* publishes this report:

> Electors across the country voted amid threats of violence and the continued, unsubstantiated allegations by President Donald Trump that he lost the November election as the result of widespread election fraud [. . .].
>
> The Michigan State Capitol was closed due to "credible threats of violence," *The Washington Post* reported, while in Arizona, the vote was held in an undisclosed location for safety reasons, according to *The New York Times*.
>
> In Wisconsin, electors were instructed to enter the capitol grounds through an "unmarked side door" to avoid protesters, as electors in the state reported having received threats of harm against them and their families if they followed through with their pledged votes for Biden.
>
> Trump has consistently stoked the anger of his supporters, tweeting this weekend that swing states "CANNOT LEGALLY CERTIFY these votes as complete & correct without committing a severely punishable crime." The president has continued to advance allegations of election fraud that have been discredited in the more than 50 court cases he and his allies have lost in seeking to overturn the results of the November election.

On Friday, the U.S. Supreme Court decided not to hear a case filed by the state of Texas and joined by the Trump campaign and publicly supported by 126 House Republicans that sought to have the results of the presidential balloting in Pennsylvania, Georgia, Michigan and Wisconsin declared unconstitutional and effectively hand Trump a second term.

Though there remains active litigation in courts wherein the Trump campaign and its allies are seeking to decertify results in many of the same battleground states, the Supreme Court's refusal to even hear the Texas case represents a comprehensive rebuke of theories of widespread voter fraud or illegal changes to state election law as factoring into the Trump loss to Biden.[116]

The next day, on the 15th of December, Kenneth Garger of the *New York Post* reports:

A former Houston Police Department captain was arrested Tuesday for allegedly pointing a gun at an air conditioner repairman he thought was orchestrating a massive voter fraud scheme, prosecutors said.

Mark Aguirre, 63, was charged with aggravated assault with a deadly weapon for the Oct. 19 confrontation, according to the Harris County District Attorney's Office.

Aguirre, a member of a group of private citizens conducting their own probe into an alleged ballot scheme, rammed his SUV into the man's work truck—believing the victim was hauling around 750,000 fraudulent ballots, prosecutors said.

The former cop then pointed his handgun at the technician when he exited his vehicle and forced him to the ground, according to prosecutors.

The day of the incident, Aguirre received $211,400 from Houston-based Liberty Center for God and Country. The group's CEO is well-known right-wing activist Steven Hotze, *The Texas Tribune* reported.

Inside the man's work truck, police found air conditioning parts and tools, not ballots, prosecutors said.[117]

★

On December 18, Rick sends me (or Ed Poe) a bizarre email letting me know that he and his "Christian Patriot" friends have petitioned "the Lord in his Courts against the Cabal/'The Enemy' on behalf of all human beings" in the form of a rambling, twelve-page, single-spaced screed he calls the "Courts of Heaven" document.

In a sense, it's intended to be a magical sigil in written form, the purpose of which is to manifest the beliefs of QAnon into physical reality.

Here are just a few excerpts:

IN THE HIGHEST COURT OF THE GOD OF ALL CREATION AND EL ELYON, THE JUST AND RIGHTEOUS JUDGE

APPEAL TO HEAVEN AS A CLASS ACTION LAWSUIT & WRIT OF HABEAS CORPUS

THE PEOPLE OF GOD WHO ARE CALLED BY HIS NAME, HIS EKKLESIA, on behalf of all living beings on our planet EARTH, and in our MILKY WAY GALAXY that are in agreement and in service to God. This also includes our ancestors, our forefathers, and our descendants.

Appellants, vs.

SOPHIA, LUCIFER et. al., ASMODEUS, CORII, AZAZEL, ABRAXAS, NOG, NUIT, THELMA, LOKI, MOG, METATRON, AND ALL PRINCIPALITIES, POWERS, THE RULERS OF THE DARKNESS OF THIS AGE, SPIRITUAL HOSTS OF WICKEDNESS IN THE HEAVENLY PLACES, THE CABAL, NEGATIVE NON-TERRESTRIALS WHO ARE NOT IN BEST INTERESTS OF ALL LIFE EVERYWHERE, [also known as The Enemies]

Appellees.

WE COME IN GOD'S HIGHEST COURT, FOR THIS COURT TO HEAR THIS APPEAL
FORGIVE ALL OUR INDIVIDUAL SINS, KNOWN AND UNKNOWN, FORGIVE THE KNOWN AND UNKNOWN SINS OF ALL GOD'S EKKLESIA, AND HEAL OUR LANDS.

As God, our Highest Judge has said in Psalm 89:14 "RIGHTEOUSNESS AND JUSTICE ARE THE FOUNDATION OF YOUR THRONE."

Your Word promises in **II Chronicles 7:14** that You will grant relief in the form of: (1) a hearing, (2) forgiveness and (3) healing of lands on the absolute condition that we, Your People: (1) humble ourselves, (2) petition You in specific prayer, (3) Seek Your Face, and (4) turn from our wicked ways.

AND as Your HOLY GOSPEL further teaches us:
In John 18 You Will Defend And Avenge Your Elect.

[. . .]

WE FURTHER BRING FORWARD the testimony of YOUR true prophets, that YOU, THE ONE TRUE GOD of ALL CREATION, Love, Light and Compassion, have anointed President Donald J. Trump, as YOUR servant, for such a time as this, in his role as the 45th President of and for these United States of America for two con-secutive terms and additional terms as appointed by YOU. Given these prophecies, the Appellees are prevented from any plans to change what You have decreed for Your anointed, Donald J. Trump to accomplish in YOUR NAME. Therefore, these United States of and for America, will reach its highest destiny, and fulfill YOUR Will. As America goes, so goes the world; the Appellees have clearly stepped outside their jurisdiction, by constantly trying to stop Your will from being done.

WE FURTHER BRING FORWARD the testimony of Q, the Q Team, and the ALLIANCE, as evidence that the Appellees have over-stepped their jurisdiction at this time. Your anointed, Donald J. Trump, Q+, set in motion the complete eradication of HUMAN TRAFFICKING (POTUS's Executive Orders) which includes, the saving of our children, adults, and all other living beings, including animals, through the clearing of the DUMBs, underground caves, tunnels, etc., on Earth. This evidence proves beyond a reasonable doubt that the Appellees have lost all jurisdiction to all their evil plans and crimes.

REVOCATION OF ALL ACTS OF THE APPELLEES

THEREFORE, WE DECREE AND DECLARE that ALL acts NOT IN SERVICE TO GOD'S CREATION: whether on EARTH, or carried out in our MILKY WAY GALAXY, are DECEPTIVE AND ILLEGAL MANEUVERS against the Appellants and those they represent.

WE DECREE AND DECLARE that all evil, demonic, criminal acts and plans of the Appellees be stopped immediately, revoked, and repealed, in all realities, on all timelines, and in every direction of time.

FOR FURTHER CLARITY, all these illegal acts and plans of the enemy that are referred to in the above paragraph includes [sic], but is not limited to:

1. ELECTION FRAUD: in any way, at any time, in ALL NATIONS on EARTH, and in this particular time, the massive fraud and cheating in the election of November 3rd, 2020, in these United States of America;

FURTHERMORE, ANY support of this massive fraud by those who were complicit in any way, in part or in whole; those who were willfully blind to the truth that Donald J. Trump won this latest election; this includes any media complicit with this fraud;

WE BOLDY [sic] submit that these shenanigans, masquerades, and complete absurdities, were done ILLEGALLY by the Appellees. Since Sidney Powell released the Kraken on Earth, we join in the spirit with her and release the Kraken of Justice and Righteousness in the Heavenly Realms.
Matthew 12:29; 16:19; 18:18. 1 Corinthians 15:46

2. THE NWO and the "Plan-demic" are ILLEGAL MOVES by the Appellees:

- the premeditated creation of a deadly virus, including taking away of human rights by mandatory mask mandates,
- lockdowns, emotional damage, especially to children,
- mandatory vaccines, loss of jobs, loss of businesses,
- promoting and/or conjuring fear in people: suicides, loss of social connection, social distancing mandates that mirror satanic rituals, isolation (e.g., refusal to allow family near deathbeds and funerals),
- lies about the plan-demic by ANYONE, including the medical community and the public health officials: fake covid numbers, fake tests and contaminated tests with the man-made virus, and any other nefarious plans of the enemies,
- whistle blowers, i.e., doctors, nurses and others who were threatened or lost their livelihood;
- censorship of truth, regarding prevention, treatments and cures;
- withholding of cures and effective treatments;
- knowingly misusing technology to cause harm going against the medical and political oaths they took;
- pharmaceutical companies that knowingly colluded in the plan-demic

[. . .]

WE DECREE AND DECLARE all other soul traps, in existence, known to GOD, ARE ILLEGAL and NULL AND VOID, as these soul traps are totally NOT in service to God's Creation.

These other soul traps that harvest God's souls, and illegally use these precious souls to manipulate, alter, and change God's will for these souls, are an abomination. As an example, these souls, harvested by any or all of the Appellees, are illegally altered by changing their GOD GIVEN heterosexual nature that is, to be a fully heterosexual male or fully a heterosexual female.

God's will and creation has no other "sexual categories" for these souls brought to Earth, other than what God intends.

WE DECREE AND DECLARE these soul traps be DESTROYED, REPEALED AND REVOKED on all timelines, in all realities, for all-time, and all directions of time, by God Almighty, our HIGHEST JUDGE.

WE DECREE AND DECLARE that with the end of these soul traps, all souls captured are released to God and restored to YOUR will, Most High Judge.

[. . .]

WE DECREE AND DECLARE that complete restoration and resti-tution be done, by the Appellees, for all demonic, illegal, and evil plans and acts that were done to the Appellants and to those on behalf of whom the Appellants appear in this Appeal to Heaven.

WE RESPECTFULLY REQUEST, therefore, that AN ORDER OF

RESTORATION AND RESTITUTION, covering all timelines, all real-ties, AND IN ALL DIRECTIONS OF TIME from YOUR THRONE BE FILED AGAINST THE APPELLEES, according to YOUR will. MAY YOUR WILL BE DONE, ON EARTH AND IN THIS MILKY WAY GALAXY, AS IT IS IN HEAVEN:

With eternal gratitude, we humbly thank the Judge of the Highest Court of Heaven, our Abba Father, for hearing this Appeal filed as a class action suit, and Writ of Habeas Corpus.

Thy Kingdom come, Thy will be done, on Earth as it is in Heaven. As it is written, so let it be done, and sealed now and for all time.

RESPECTFULLY SUBMITTED:

Blessed To Teach and Serve Ekklesia

Dated this 18 day of December in the Year of our Lord, 2020.

★

Two days later, Rick is back in the studio advertising his new "Gene Unleashed" t-shirt, which features the slogan, "The Choice To Know Will Be YOURS." Apparently, evangelical Christians are "pro-choice" only when it comes to accepting transparently ludicrous disinformation campaigns with no critical thinking whatsoever. (You can buy the t-shirt from his online store if you're interested—it's your choice, of course.)

After this blatant plug, Rick informs us, "There's no *two* parties right now! It's evil or it's truth. It's evil or it's good! And that is becoming *extremely* clear right now. There're many Republicans who've chosen to stay with the evil, to fall and be intimidated, when this is the time to *fight*. Here we have Donald Trump saying [on Twitter], 'The lie of the year is that Joe Biden won!' [. . .] So here we are at the end of the year— you're lookin' back. What's the lie of the year? It's that Joe Biden won! [Laughs] And of course they put the notice here [from] the criminal thought police of Twitter, 'Election officials have certified Joe Biden as the winner of the U.S. Presidential election.' [Laughs again] The fact is that there is *no* President-elect until January 6th . . . in a contested election. Obviously, if everybody said, 'Oh, we lost, you won, you're the President-elect,' that's one thing. But this is contested. This is *completely* contested! And so January 6th is a big day. Now, could we see a lot evidence come out *after* January 6th, and turmoil, and potential military action? Potentially. But I think there's obviously a good chance that our Constitution might come through here despite the corruption of all these judges down in the lower state areas, despite the fact that they haven't looked at anything based on merit and are trying to use some procedural [. . .] excuse for not enforcing the remedy. Right? The fact is that the amount of voter fraud is overwhelming. And there's more coming. Almost every day there's huge amounts of new evidence, and I even believe there's going to be more, particularly if you look at the prophecies of Amanda over the last couple of months."

A few minutes later, Gene joins Rick for yet another epistemological discussion:

Gene: "My life now seems like I'm living every sci-fi movie and fantasy movie and book I've ever read simultaneously [. . .]. What we think is normal is not at all. They [the Illuminati] have known many, many, many things that seem to us like utter fantasy. As most people realize, as you go down the rabbit hole, you go, 'Can this *really* be true?' I mean, it seems like this is some *movie* I saw!"

Rick: "I think it's good, though—don't you, Gene?—that we're getting people away from the lies of the media. They're trying to pull us into this timeline of Joe Biden becoming the President when we know that's not what we're accepting, and we're fighting against that, and we know that's *not* going to happen."

Gene: "I don't care how big the person is, how many followers they have—in the hundreds of millions or whatever. You don't see Trump pumping fear. Anytime you have somebody who's fearmongering, pumping and misleading you—even if there's some tragic events that have happened, [Trump] leaves you with a note at the end of *hope*. And that things will be better. The best is yet to come. You want somebody who's planting your feet in faith and in hope, and not focusing you on the dark side of things. Fear is the opposite of faith."[118]

Pause for a moment and meditate on the irony of this fellow spending the last few years of his life obtaining international notoriety via the internet by peddling hours upon hours of horror stories—with no verifiable evidence whatsoever—about thousands upon thousands of innocent children being dragged down into hellish grottoes located beneath America where they're brutally violated by high-ranking initiates of the Illuminati (many of whom are, according to Gene, revered politicians and entertainers) and then promptly stuffed down the gullets of ancient, Lovecraftian Elder Gods, turning around and chastising members of the mainstream media for "fearmongering"?

In Gene's mind, the idea of Trump losing the 2020 election is infinitely more terrifying than ten thousand kids disappearing down the throat of a giant demon.

★

A day later, on December 21, KPTV in Oregon reports:

A protest outside of the Oregon State Capitol during a special legislative session Monday ended with four arrests and one person being sought, according to Oregon State Patrol.

OSP said the group gathered at 8:30 a.m. and attempted to enter the building, which was closed to the public due to the pandemic. The group was heard chanting "open up" – signaling their support for loosening Oregon's COVID-19 restrictions.

Several protesters gained access to the building as a person left the building. Troopers asked them to go, and "the altercation became physical."

One of the protesters sprayed some kind of chemical irritant or bear spray into the vestibule, but Troopers and Salem police were able to contain the crowd.

OSP said that despite several warnings to leave or face arrest for trespassing, protesters stayed. At 10:30 a.m., a protester sprayed a chemical irritant again at police leading to [the arrest of] Ryan Lyles, 41 [. . .]. Lyles was charged with being a felon in possession of body armor and unlawful use of mace.

Protesters also deployed a device that emitted smoke during the engagement, according to OSP.

Two people identified as Ronald Vanvlack, 75, and Jerry Dyerson, 53, refused to leave the building and were taken into custody, OSP said. They were charged with criminal trespass and disorderly conduct.

At about 1:30 p.m., a man, identified as Jeremiah Pruitt, 35, attempted to gain entry on the west side of the Capitol building by breaking a window of one of the doors, according to OSP. Pruitt was arrested and charged with criminal mischief and disorderly conduct.

OSP is searching for Jeremy Roberts, 40, who is believed to have attempted to enter the building that afternoon and may have attacked two reporters.

Many in the crowd were seen holding Trump signs, while others were openly carrying weapons

Despite the group's efforts, the Oregon legislature concluded the special session and passed four COVID relief bills.[119]

★

Meanwhile, on that same day, Gene returns to Rick's show to reveal the full details of his origin story and the wellsprings of his most sensitive and Above Top Secret information. According to Gene, he depends upon two vital sources: 1) the voice of "God" and 2) "spies."

Gene: "[God] actually told me that I had to get His Word out. He allowed me to come back from a thirty-minute death experience to help Him for the Great Awakening and to wake up the world and to keep all of the human race on the highest timeline of His Divine Plan [. . .]. God told me to do the D.U.M.B. [Deep Underground Military Base] decode. The world had to know where they [the Illuminati] were doing these things to the children because the focus of humanity had to wake up to what was being done beneath their feet, where they were planning their NWO [New World Order] movement, to go into those [bases] after they had wiped us off the surface of the Earth with all our children they'd taken and harvest them and keep harvesting various things through horrific means. That curtain *had* to be pulled aside [. . .].

"God would say, 'Go here and type in this.' When I first found Q—the first Q, back in 2017 on 4chan—I was out working on my back deck and He just told me, 'Blow the sawdust off with the leaf blower as much as you can and go up and bring up computer-type stuff on the keyboard.' I don't even know—I'm tech-challenged beyond belief—I don't know how I did it. You know, it's just God's direction. Same with the D.U.M.B. decode, the first one. A lot of it is just, you know, God telling me where to go to look for things and what to type in [. . .]. It took six months to get that first connection. It was bizarre when it happened. It was very subtle. I literally felt a tap on my shoulder and [heard] a whisper in my ear: 'You're welcome.' Very shortly after that, the connection became quite strong. As you continue to go there every day, you can literally have full-out conversations [with God]. I've gotten chemical formulas, quantum equations, differential equations, pages and pages, all kinds of things. So this was exactly that type of thing where, along with the time it takes to do the research—the primary thing was the thirty years of research when I first red-pilled back in 1990, when I originally started. I was spending every Friday afternoon when I got off work till Sunday when they close [at] the Supreme Court law library [. . .]. Because we train that way in the military—to study, or stand watch, long maneuvering marches, battle stations, etc., so I had that kind of stamina. I was in great shape with my martial arts, so I would literally study for more than forty-eight hours straight, going to the Supreme Court law library, Congressional registers, following the money, Executive Orders, obscure documents, all that kind of thing as well. And then taking courses and learning more and more, and researching, and asking God for information, and then getting to [the point where] God would just bring people [to me]. I got to meet people like Dr. [John] Coleman who wrote *The Committee of Three Hundred*, and many, many fine, cutting-edge persons that helped me get information, as well as some spies who came—literally, just *showed* up in my life! It's literally, like, the force of God brings people to you when you're trying to help and be in service to Him."[120]

Let's play that sentence back for a moment: "Some spies who came—literally, just *showed* up in my life!"

Back in 1987, Robert Anton Wilson wrote the following gnomic words:

> In CIA jargon, a "useful idiot" means somebody who is working for them but doesn't know it.

> My involvements with controversial politics have left me with one lasting legacy. Whenever I suspect that I am taking myself or my theories too seriously, I stop and ask myself, "Have I become a useful idiot yet?"[121]

These are words that Gene should definitely consider, though I doubt he's ever read them . . . or ever will read them.

Unless he somehow reads this book.

But that can't happen because he will never read anything not written by those who haven't yet accepted the light and salvation offered by the seventeenth letter of the alphabet into their furry little freakish hearts.

★

The next day, the 22nd of December, Ben Collins of NBC News publishes a report entitled "As Trump Meets with QAnon Influencers, the Conspiracy's Adherents Beg for Dictatorship":

> On Friday, President Donald Trump met with current and former advisers in the Oval Office, including retired Lt. Gen. Michael Flynn, and a person familiar with the meeting said Flynn advocated an extreme way to overturn the November election: declare martial law.
>
> The idea is hardly limited to Flynn, Trump's disgraced former national security adviser. It has also been embraced by the QAnon movement and some members of the Republican Party.
>
> With Trump's days in office dwindling, QAnon influencers have become increasingly restless and militant, urging him to #crosstherubicon, a reference to Julius Caesar's crossing the Rubicon river after the Roman Senate explicitly

told him not to, effectively kick-starting the Roman civil war and Caesar's dictatorship.

Arizona Republican Party Chairwoman Kelli Ward tweeted the hashtag Sunday.

"Mr. President @realDonaldTrump - we are with you in #Arizona. We are working every avenue to stop this coup & to stop our Republic from crumbing [sic]," she tweeted. "Patriots are united. Those who are against us are exposing themselves. #Liberty & #freedom are on the line. #CrossTheRubicon @GenFlynn."

Trump tweeted Sunday that reports of a discussion about martial law were "knowingly bad reporting."

"Martial law = Fake news," he wrote.

But that hasn't dampened the enthusiasm for military rule from the QAnon community, which sees hope in the fact that some of their central influencers are close to Trump.

Sidney Powell, a lawyer who has filed a series of suits she dubbed "the Kraken," which have failed to overturn the results of the election in several states, was part of the meeting. She has repeatedly pushed QAnon theories, and she has used the hashtag #TheStormIsComing, a QAnon phrase that refers to the extrajudicial roundup of Democrats at the heart of the theory.

Flynn, a hero in the mythology of the QAnon conspiracy theory who once took a QAnon "oath" on video, has said in appearances on the conservative media channel Newsmax that Trump should use the military to "rerun" the election.[122]

Just in case there's anyone alive on planet Earth who's still unclear about Trump's true loyalties, the same day the previous article appears, President Kek pardons four Blackwater guards responsible for massacring fourteen innocent Iraqi civilians back in 2007.

Blackwater, a private military company now known as Academi, is owned by Erik Prince, the brother of Trump's education secretary, Betsy DeVos.

Laurel Wamsley of NPR News reports:

> Among the pardons made by President Trump this week, the pardon of four former guards for Blackwater was regarded by some as particularly galling.
>
> Nicholas Slatten, Paul Slough, Evan Liberty and Dustin Heard were convicted six years ago of killing 14 Iraqi civilians and wounding 17 others. Witnesses described how the American men ambushed the civilians unprovoked, firing on Baghdad's Nisour Square with heavy gunfire and grenade launchers.
>
> The massacre took place in 2007, when the four were working as guards for Blackwater, a private military contractor, on an assignment in Baghdad. They claimed they were fired on, but prosecutors said the Blackwater guards opened fire first. Slatten, whom prosecutors said started the shooting, was sentenced to life in prison.
>
> Hassan Salman is among the Iraqis shot during the ambush. He told NPR on Wednesday that he was shocked by Trump's pardons—he himself had made trips to the U.S. to give testimony in the proceedings against the four.
>
> "Today we were surprised that the American president issued a decision to pardon these criminals, murderers and thugs," Salman said, speaking from Baghdad. "I'm really shocked. . . . The American judiciary is fair and equitable. I had never imagined that Trump or any other politician would affect American justice."[123]

One might argue that "American justice" is exactly what Trump meted out when he decided to pardon four bloodthirsty mercenaries hired to enforce George W. Bush's neocon Iraqi war—a war that Trump once claimed was based on a "lie."[124]

On Christmas morning, three days following these pardons, which "violate U.S. obligations under international law and more broadly undermine humanitarian law and human rights at a global level"[125] (according to Jelena Aparac, chair of the United States working group on the use of mercenaries), a sixty-three-year-old computer tech named Anthony Quinn Warner parks his RV outside the AT&T building in Nashville, Tennessee and blows himself up, injuring three people and destroying a large section of the city's downtown area, including "a key AT&T transmission facility." According to *The Verge*, this act "brought down wireless and wired networks across parts of Tennessee, Kentucky, and Alabama—disrupting cell service, some 911 networks, and communications at the Nashville International Airport, which briefly grounded flights as a result."[126]

The second I hear about the bombing, I think, "Okay . . . just sit back and wait for the QAnon connection." Within a couple of days, Ben Ashford of the *Daily Mail* reports:

> Nashville bomber Anthony Quinn Warner hoped he would be "hailed a hero" for targeting AT&T because he believed 5G cellular technology was killing people, DailyMail.com can exclusively reveal.
>
> The 63-year-old computer tech—who died in the suspected suicide blast but was identified Sunday from DNA found in his mangled RV—was "heavily into conspiracy theories," according to a source close to the investigation.
>
> Various baseless theories have circulated since the lightning-fast 5G network was introduced, some claiming it's a tool to spy on Americans, others speculating that it has fueled the spread of COVID-19.[127]

The latter theory, of course, has circulated most prominently through the internet among QAnon acolytes since the beginning of the national lockdown in March of 2020.

The High Weirdness amps up in Rick's studio on January 2, 2021, when Gene arrives to explain the "true" story behind Anthony Quinn Warner's explosive death:

Gene: "They [Trump's white hats] took the Dominion machines and the [CIA] server hardware and software from these raids in Madrid, Nice, and Frankfurt, and they downloaded everything [. . .]. They had it all gone out of [Nashville] two days before the Cabal operation. So Trump's sitting there laughing in the White House at them with their bomb trying to blow up and create [. . .] a crater where Nashville was. That's why it was a no-fly zone. The [Alliance] came in with a TR7 while the Cabal put a graphite bomb in the basement and [told an] expert from the [CIA to] go in there and start the timer. He'd learned from the Oklahoma City situation. He rebuilt the timer, so he thought he could get out of there. So the Cabal then [used] a laser, 'cause they don't even have good weapons anymore. They're down to the low stuff. They hit the device with a laser instead to do the detonation that would float that gas [. . .], which is eighty percent as powerful as a nuclear blast. That's what we also saw in Beirut, Lebanon, which turned the Marine barracks into a crater. They wanted to do that to say if we don't put Biden in, they're gonna do something—a 9/11 event that makes that look pale. 'We're gonna make Nashville a crater!' It's hitting at the heart of the *music*. It's literally hitting at the frequency of God! That's what they wanted to show."

Rick: "Wow!"

Gene: "Yeah."

Rick: "So we were able to keep away from a disaster then?"

Gene: "A *horrific* disaster. I mean, imagine all of Nashville gone. A crater. Let alone the earthquake that would, you know, go across the country. The devastation would have been massive."

Rick: "So . . . we had a TR3B come in and save *us*?"

Gene: "A TR7. What they did is, they flew in and once that gas had started to expand outward they did a reverse compression particle wave that caused it to ignite and feedback on itself and compress itself. A compression explosion [. . .] took out the RV that [the CIA agent] came in, along with the RV that shot the laser. So that's why you had two RV's there. It took out both of them! And of course that guy [the CIA agent] was trying to get into his RV and leave, so he was taken out too. All of that was completely empty. All that was there was just a bunch of empty servers [that were used to switch votes from Trump to Biden] that had already been downloaded, and Trump's watching the whole thing in the White House laughing at the Cabal. These people are *stupid!* Just like they did to us, tapped all our phones and everything [. . .], the NSA has it all. They tapped *all* the Cabal stuff! So they have military members in all their organizations. They infiltrated us, so we did the same thing. We infiltrated *them!*"

Gene also regales the faithful with this most peculiar State of the Union speech:

"The entire U.S. military is on high alert. Trump has called back massive amounts of military assets and stationed three carrier groups off the West Coast and two off the East Coast. One of these groups just took out two D.U.M.B.s—the first in Canada on the border of Michigan and the second on the border of Maine where fifty thousand Chinese troops were poised to invade the U.S. and all were destroyed with 50k ton yield bunker buster bombs! The 82nd Airborne is poised for an operation. This is the group that General [Michael] Flynn and AG [Richard] Donoghue were from. [Trump] has defunded the CIA. He just removed [Henry] Kissinger and [Madeleine] Albright from the National Security Advisory Board and replaced them with men loyal to him. These positions were created as part of the treaty when the U.S. lost and surrendered to the Nazis after the battle of Antarctica/Operation High Jump. This means that POTUS has removed not only the ancient satanic control over the U.S. but also that of the Nazis! All the pieces are in place and POTUS has it *all*! He is just waiting for the timing. He knows he won and they committed treason. *Nothing* can stop what's coming!"

You would think the above would be enough excitement for one night, but Gene's not done yet. In fact, he's just getting warmed up. You see, for an extra fee, one can purchase a "backstage pass" that enables the elite members of the audience to communicate with Rick and Gene via Zoom before, during, and after the show. All throughout Gene's monologue, we can see on his screen a handful of Rick and Gene's most devout followers. All of them appear to be elderly White people, many of them with red, white, and blue Trump campaign signs hanging on the walls behind them. When Gene reveals that Trump was laughing at the Cabal for screwing up their "stupid" attempt to turn Nashville into a crater, an elderly man pumps both fists in the air in triumph. An old woman claps her hands together like a giddy child at a birthday party . . .

. . . despite the fact that Gene has presented the audience with *zero* evidence that any of this has occurred. When I was a child, my parents presented me with more convincing evidence for the existence of Santa Claus than these full-grown adults have been given for the *entirety* of the QAnon scenario (much less the thwarted extinction of Nashville), and yet they choose to swallow it all without a moment of doubt.

Double fist pump.

Tiny hand clap.

★

Intermission.

A spotlight from the rafters shines down on a beautiful young woman wearing a sequined one-piece who sashays across the stage while holding above her head a large red, white, and blue cardboard sign that reads:

"The two most common elements in the universe are Hydrogen and stupidity."
—Harlan Ellison

The spotlight shuts off abruptly, casting the stage in darkness. A brief moment of silence follows.

★

Gene then expounds on the significance of January 6 to the thousands of Christians hanging on his every word.

Gene: "They've been doing this same thing [election fraud] all over the world for almost a century. We haven't been getting—unless they *wanted* that person—the person we vote for for over a century, anywhere on Earth. So, you know, January 6th is not about the political future of Trump. It's about the future of the human race and the Earth. We have been given to us by God inalienable rights, and that's the right to life, liberty, and the pursuit of happiness, and that when we vote we get our vote the way we put our vote, not what *they* want! It's not about what *they* want. It's about what *we* want! Sheep no more! *We're* the lions. And as the Bible reads, at this time, on this timeline, the lion shall lay [sic] down with the wolf. This is the wolf in sheep's clothing: the Cabal. If you're going to behave yourself, and be kind and considerate and respectful and do the law of God, *thee* God of all Creation, the *only* God of all Creation, and the law of the country you're in, as per the people that put that law in, not your elite, but the people themselves—[if] you're going to uphold that, we will lay [sic] down with you. But if you don't want to do that, then you're either gonna need to *surrender* or we'll take you to a military tribunal or a court system, and if you won't do that, and you're doing things to children and all these other things, we'll arrange a meeting for you with the God of all Creation and the highest court in existence, the court of *God*! So, that being said, January 6th is extremely important."

Then Gene tells his audience to relax if they happen to see tank armadas rolling down their city streets on the 6th of January: "If you're getting freaked out, don't. Faith, not fear. If you're in a lockdown, stay inside and stay out of the way. Let the military do what they need to do [. . .]. We know Trump won the popular vote, as well as over 410 Electoral College votes. We knew he won, and we'll see him elected on the 20th of January, 2021."[128]

Why is Gene so confident when relating these stories? Is it because he's a master class actor? Somehow I doubt it. It sounds to me like he believes all of these things, that these tall tales originate from a source well outside Gene's limited imagination. I suspect he implicitly trusts the word of the people whose job it is to *feed* him these scenarios. Who could such people be? Are they the "spies" he mentioned before, the ones who fortuitously "showed up" in his life around the same time that Q started posting on 4chan?

★

The next day (Sunday, January 3, 2021), *The Washington Post* publishes an exclusive report about President Trump desperately attempting to coerce Brad Raffensperger, the Georgia secretary of state, to "find" new votes for the express purpose of flipping the election in Trump's favor. This "flagrant abuse of power" (a description used by legal scholars quoted by the *Post*) occurs during an hour-long phone conversation, the entire recording of which is made available on the *Post's* website. There's little doubt that this is a criminal act on Trump's part.

The following is from Amy Gardner's January 3, 2021 *Washington Post* article entitled "'I Just Want to Find 11,780 Votes': In Extraordinary Hour-long Call, Trump Pressures Georgia Secretary of State to Recalculate the Vote in His Favor":

> *The Washington Post* obtained a recording of the conversation in which Trump alternately berated Raffensperger, tried to flatter him, begged him to act and threatened him with vague criminal consequences if the secretary of state refused to pursue his false claims, at one point warning that Raffensperger was taking "a big risk."
>
> Throughout the call, Raffensperger and his office's general counsel rejected Trump's assertions, explaining that the president is relying on debunked conspiracy theories and that President-elect Joe Biden's 11,779-vote victory in Georgia was fair and accurate.
>
> Trump dismissed their arguments.
>
> "The people of Georgia are angry, the people of the country are angry," he said. "And there's nothing wrong with saying, you know, that you've recalculated."
>
> Raffensperger responded: "Well, Mr. President, the challenge that you have is, the data you have is wrong."[129]

While listening to this extremely weird phone conversation, and hearing the tone of Trump's voice, it occurs to me that Trump *sincerely believes* the 2020 presidential election was rigged. It's not just an act on his part. Based on this phone call, it's clear that Trump has been listening to the very same QAnon conspiracy theorists he and his reelection team probably subsidized and/or encouraged in the first place. The implications are mindboggling. Does this mean that Trump listens to Rick and Gene on *The B2T Show* and thinks, "Is *that* what I'm up to? Did I *really* save thousands of kids from underground gulags? I guess I did do that, and I just don't remember it. Man, I'm such a good guy. Am I really the Anointed One? Who would want to vote against the Anointed One? No one! So the election results *must* be faked!"

Here's a crucial excerpt from the transcript:

Trump: I won this election by hundreds of thousands of votes. There's no way I lost Georgia. There's no way. We won by hundreds of thousands of votes. I'm just going by small numbers, when you add them up, they're many times the 11,000. But I won that state by hundreds of thousands of votes. Do you think it's possible that they shredded ballots in Fulton County? Because that's what the rumor is. And also that Dominion took out machines. That Dominion is really moving fast to get rid of their, uh, machinery. Do you know anything about that? Because that's illegal, right?

Germany: This is Ryan Germany [Raffensperger's lawyer]. No, Dominion has not moved any machinery out of Fulton County.

Trump: But have they moved the inner parts of the machines and replaced them with other parts?

Germany: No.

Trump: Are you sure, Ryan?

Germany: I'm sure. I'm sure, Mr. President.

Trump: What about, what about the ballots? The shredding of the ballots. Have they been shredding ballots?

Germany: The only investigation that we have into that—they have not been shredding any ballots. There was an issue in Cobb County where they were doing normal office shredding, getting rid of old stuff, and we investigated that. But this stuff from—you know, from, you know, past elections.

Trump: It doesn't pass the smell test because we hear they're shredding thousands and thousands of ballots, and now what they're saying, "Oh, we're just cleaning up the office." You know.

Raffensperger: Mr. President, the problem you have with social media, they—people can say anything.

Trump: Oh this isn't social media . . . this is *Trump* media![130]

Bingo. Abracadabra Alakazam. There it is. *Trump* media. With the utterance of those two magical words, all known boundaries of rationality dissolve. The ultimate post–postmodern moment. The Omega Point, as predicted by Catholic priest Pierre Teilhard de Chardin in the 1950s. The immanentizing of the Eschaton, as predicted by the *Principia Discordia* in the 1960s. The Timewave Zero singularity, as predicted by Terence McKenna in the 1970s. The moment when Ouroboros collapses in upon itself and vanishes into another plane of existence.

Not social media. *Trump* media. Not disinformation. *Truth*. Not evil. *Good*. Not "Where We Go One, We Go All." *Trump*, representing himself and no one else. A mythological serpent with Trump's head consumes its own tail as it sits coiled in the front row of a packed carnival tent eagerly awaiting the next act in

Cooger & Dark's Pandemonium QAnon Show. A dog drops its tail, spins around, bows its head, and awaits the tail's commands. A ventriloquist takes a break from his own roadshow attraction and watches the limp puppet sitting there on the stage, waiting for it to move, wondering why it refuses to get up on its wooden feet and do a little dance. Who is the master and who is the puppet?

Is it possible that Trump understood the QAnon phenomenon was a strategically created disinformation campaign and then somehow *forgot* it? Is it possible that Trump's Operation Mindfuck has boomeranged back on him and screwed up his own mind? Is it possible that Trump popped a little blue pill he himself manufactured?

Is Donald Trump just the latest dupe in his own psychological warfare campaign?

If so, he wouldn't be the first politician to swallow his own lies.

Or perhaps this is just another act of flamboyant public theater to lay the groundwork for the reality TV show that is sure to follow Trump's eviction from the White House.

★

The day after Trump's phone call with Raffensperger, all ten living secretaries of defense publish an op-ed piece in *The Washington Post* in which they warn, "Efforts to involve the U.S. armed forces in resolving election disputes would take us into dangerous, unlawful and unconstitutional territory. Civilian and military officials who direct or carry out such measures would be accountable, including potentially facing criminal penalties, for the grave consequences of their actions on our republic."[131]

One of the authors of the piece is William Cohen, who served as Secretary of Defense in the Clinton administration from 1997 to 2001. In a January 4, 2021 NPR article entitled "In

Op-Ed, 10 Ex-Defense Secretaries Say Military Has No Role In Election Dispute," reporter Jaclyn Diaz writes:

> [William] Cohen, who represented Maine as a Republican U.S. senator for almost 20 years, said he is concerned Trump is attempting to promote civil unrest as justification to deploy military forces in the streets.
>
> "There are things taking place which pose, I think, a threat to our domestic tranquility and security, and that is the president encouraging some of the more right-wing extremists to march on Washington and to protest," Cohen said. "And the indication is he's urging them to—it's going to be wild."[132]

★

Two days later, Congress meets to certify Joe Biden as President-elect. In the middle of this process, at Trump's urging, an angry mob composed of hundreds of his supporters attack the Capitol Building in Washington, D.C., resulting in the deaths of five people and over seven hundred arrests.

Ted Barrett, Manu Raju, and Peter Nickeas of CNN report:

> The stunning display of insurrection was the first time the US Capitol had been overrun since the British attacked and burned the building in August of 1814, during the War of 1812, according to Samuel Holliday, director of scholarship and operations with the US Capitol Historical Society.
>
> The shocking scene was met with less police force than many of the Black Lives Matter protests that rolled across the country in the wake of George Floyd's killing at the hands of Minneapolis police officers last year. While federal police attacked peaceful protesters in Lafayette Square outside the White House over the summer, clearing the way for Trump to take a photo in front of a nearby church at the time,

protesters on Wednesday were able to overrun Capitol police and infiltrate the country's legislative chambers.[133]

Some suggest the Washington, D.C. police were ordered not to engage with the protestors simply to prevent handing Trump an excuse to declare martial law and thus delay the inauguration of Joe Biden—perhaps the entire reason Trump urged the insurrection in the first place.

Among the rioters are numerous QAnon acolytes. In his January 6, 2021 *Daily Dot* article entitled "Major QAnon Figure Stands Atop House Chamber in Fur Costume," David Covucci reports:

> As supporters of President Donald Trump stormed the U.S. Capitol today—ending this nation's boast of two consecutive centuries of a peaceful transition of power—a QAnon supporter stood atop the dais of the House of Representatives, a symbol of a movement that has been at war with American democracy since Trump came to power.
>
> Jake Angeli, known in Q circles as the Shaman for his face paint and furs, was part of the crowd that attempted to seize the U.S. Capitol.
>
> Throughout the day numerous Q supporters were spotted in the movement that stormed the U.S. Capitol [. . .].[134]

As the events of January 6 unfold, news commentators are baffled by the paradoxical images of pro-Trump rioters wearing "BLUE LIVES MATTER" t-shirts going out of their way to clash with police officers. If you know the way QAnon followers think, however, this isn't confusing at all. QAnon followers support police officers in an *abstract sense* only. What they support is their own twisted view of law enforcement. If a police officer attempts to stop a QAnon acolyte from delaying the confirmation of Joe Biden, that officer is no longer a blue "LIFE" at all. It's a literal demon in human form or a human being who supports the rape and torture of innocent children. The officer forsakes any human attributes the second it refuses to lend its authority to the goal of keeping Trump in the White House in perpetuity.

All across the country, as horrified Americans watch enraged insurrectionists break into the Capitol Building and pursue a lone Black police officer up the stairs, people ask themselves, "Why would *anyone* behave in this way?"

Imagine: If you sincerely believed that you would be tossed into a concentration camp and your children raped by Democrats and fed to demons in the event of Biden being certified President-elect, what might *you* do?

The most logically structured argument in the history of the world will not break these people out of the alternate reality they've chosen to inhabit for the past four years.

At this stage perhaps only deprogramming, the kind sometimes administered to survivors of Scientology and other forms of cult brainwashing, could lift the veil of nonsense permanently wrapped around these people's minds.

★

It's now January 7, and Rick takes to his microphone to reveal that *all* the violent rioters in D.C. were Black Lives Matter/Antifa instigators disguised as QAnon/Trump supporters.

(I wrote the previous sentence before I even listened to Rick's November 7th broadcast. Yes, that's how predictable these people tend to be.)

The 1-6-21 insurrection, Rick insists within the first few minutes of the broadcast, was nothing more than a "False Flag" operation enacted by BLM and Antifa. He tells his audience to prepare for "civil unrest" and a military operation that will pave the way for "the Trump Administration 2.0."

"The Media will be eliminated!" he declares, grinning. "Trump's gonna work with the military and say, 'Okay, take over, here you go! I'm doing a peaceful transition of power to *you*!'" [Laughs maniacally.] "Oh, man, amazing stuff's goin' on!"

He takes a brief break to pitch his special line of B2T "survival" supplies, then swings right back into his ode to martial law.

"The military is the only way," Rick says, insisting that January 19, 2021, will be the day the U.S. military wrests control of America from the Cabal. "I don't believe they'll *wait* until after the 19th!"[135]

More dates. More commercials.

More prophecies. More promises.

Meanwhile, as Rick tries to convince his audience to invest in gold once more, a decorated Air Force veteran named Ashli Babbitt lies dead in Washington, D.C. after being shot by police for trying to storm the Capitol Building at Trump's orders. The same day Rick takes to the air to cover his ass with lies, journalists Brandy Zadrozny and Mosheh Gains of NBC report that Babbitt "was an ardent supporter of President Donald Trump and a follower and promoter of many well-known radical conservative activists as well as leaders of the QAnon conspiracy theory movement."[136]

As a reward for this military veteran's devout service to the ideals of Q and Trump, Ashli's fellow traveler, Rick Rene (who claims to be so "blessed to serve" his flock), a prominent "leader" of the QAnon movement, a man Babbitt probably respected, can't wait to scurry back into his little home studio in Texas and declare her senseless death a "False Flag."

Perhaps Q's prophecies were correct after all. QAnon's revelations did indeed shine a light on the demons lurking in the middle of a festering, morally corrupt swampland.

When the final hermetic seal is pulled aside, and the most bloated monster of them all is revealed to the masses, we will see none other than good ol' Rick squatting in the center of a fetid quagmire called "America," hypocritically sucking off the drained corpses of his loyal listeners while denying they ever existed in the first place.

"What, this inconsequential little bullet-ridden corpse?" says Rick as he sinks a pair of yellowing, elongated fangs into the pale neck of a thirty-five-year-old woman. "Oh, this lifeless thing isn't real. This is just a 'False Flag.' What your eyes *tell* you you're seeing, you're not actually seeing at all. Understand? Move on. There's nothing important happening here, my fellow Christian Patriots. You must be witnessing a wholly manufactured timeline, one the Illuminati has beamed into your head with their satanic technology." Ashli's head bobs limply as Rick digs into her bloody chest wounds with a plastic fork he picked up from Chick-fil-A.

I wonder if Ashli invested in Rick's special "survival" supplies before she chose to suck up a fusillade of bullets just so Rick wouldn't have to dirty his hands by engaging in the very course of action he and Gene have been blatantly promoting for the past three years.

As Gene himself said on Rick's show only four days before the insurrection: "You're either gonna need to *surrender* or we'll take you to a military tribunal or a court system, and if you won't do that, and you're doing things to children and all these other things, we'll arrange a meeting for you with the God of all Creation and the highest court in existence, the court of *God*!"

If that's not a threat and a call to arms, I don't know what is.

"Where We Go One, We Go All," as Rick and his Q-heads love to say . . . except when one of your comrade-in-arms is shot by a cop while committing a crime in your name, potentially sullying your ever-expanding podcast empire, and you turn your back on your fallen soldier and pretend she never even existed in the first place.

Over the course of the one hour, eight minutes, and forty seconds of *words words words* that Rick vomits into the air one night after the death of his fellow patriot, he never feels the need to mention her name even once.

According to his LinkedIn account, Rick Rene lives in the Dallas/Ft. Worth area, has a cushy tech job at IBM, and describes himself as a "Video & Podcast Host" and a "High-Performance Coach/Consultant." His specialties include "Public Speaking" and "Activating Christian Patriots."[137]

★

It's now January 10 and Rick is livestreaming with a "Back to the Basics" approach in an apparent attempt to attract new recruits. He begins the show by warning us that the "silent civil war" is "going public soon." The "silent civil war" Rick is referring to sounds suspiciously like what Charles Manson and his Family called "Helter Skelter." He then proceeds to give us a primer about Q's noble attempts to "take down" the Deep State, during which he makes the following statement: "[Q gives us] great insight to wake us up, but he also uses disinformation to confuse the Cabal. Very early posts were talking about arresting Hillary Clinton and [John] Podesta. Everybody's focus was here in the United States. In the meantime, there was a huge operation going on in Saudi Arabia and we *took out* the Cabal in Saudi Arabia!"

Rick then presents his audience with reams of evidence to support this last statement, right?

Nope.

Rick tells his audience to "think for yourselves" while continuously demanding that they take everything Q (and, by extension, Rick) says on pure faith alone. The fact that Rick has just acknowledged that Q "uses disinformation" should ring warning bells in the minds of every member of his audience.

Listen:

In October of 2002 I attended the eightieth anniversary of The Egyptian Theater in Los Angeles. To help celebrate this gala event, the American Cinematheque decided to add a little esoteric flair to the proceedings. At exactly midnight, a famous medium presided over a séance with the purpose of contacting the numerous spirits that were said to haunt the legendary theater, built back in October of 1922. Forrest J Ackerman, the late editor of *Famous Monsters of Filmland Magazine*, took part in the séance. He grew quite emotional and teary-eyed as the medium contacted (or appeared to contact) Ackerman's wife, Wendayne, who had passed away in 1990.

Just before the séance, the medium stood in the theater's center aisle and announced that he would attempt to contact the legions of ghosts rumored to still roam the Egyptian. The medium made a great show of placing his hands on his head and concentrating very hard as he attempted to penetrate the thin barrier between this world and the next. He claimed to have contacted—just recently, during other séances—several movie stars of Hollywood's Golden Age: Charlie Chaplin, Buster Keaton, James Dean, John Wayne, Marilyn Monroe, and . . .

Fay Wray.

Fay Wray, the iconic star of *King Kong* and so many other classic horror films of the 1930s: *Doctor X*, *The Most Dangerous*

Game, The Vampire Bat, The Mystery of the Wax Museum, Black Moon, etc.

Now, keep in mind that this was 2002. I remember blinking in confusion. I glanced over at my friend sitting beside me. He stared at me in bemusement.

I thought for sure I had seen Fay Wray at the Academy Awards only a few years before. I recalled Billy Crystal introducing a tribute to her film career.

I thought, Did Fay Wray die between then and now and somehow I hadn't heard about it?

Of course, the medium hadn't bothered to take something very crucial into account before accepting this gig. This was The Egyptian Theater. In Los Angeles. At midnight. On a Friday night/Saturday morning. The *only* people who would be there at that time would be hardcore movie nerds. He wasn't going to be able to get anything past these people.

Way off in the back row, I suddenly hear someone say, "Uh . . . Fay Wray's still alive."

From up in the balcony: "Yeah, Fay Wray's still alive!"

From the front row: "Oh, Fay Wray. Yeah, she's still alive! I just saw her take out her trash this morning!"

From somewhere in the middle of the theater: "Fay Wray's not dead! In fact, she's scheduled to speak here next month!"

The medium went silent for several seconds. I could see the wheels turning in his head. As a few titters of laughter began to burble through the crowd, the medium straightened up, held his palms out in front of him like Dr. Strange confronting an oncoming horde of Mindless Ones, and proclaimed, "Oh, of course. This is a very common phenomenon! You see, sometimes demons will come through the séance and *pretend* to be deceased humans! This must be what happened in this particular case, obviously."

He continued his presentation with great aplomb, not seeming flustered at all.

One side of my brain thought: Good save, dude.

The other side of my brain thought: What the holy hell? So doesn't that throw your entire worldview into question? You think you're talking to your dead Aunt Tilly, but it might *not* be your dead Aunt Tilly at all. It could be a freakin' *demon* you're talking to. So what's the point of the exercise? If a demon can pretend to be the ghost of Fay Wray while Fay Wray's still alive, they can do any damn thing they want, can't they? You could never know who or *what* you're actually communicating with.

So . . . back to Rick: Here he is, finally admitting that Q incorporates a good deal of "disinformation" into his/her/their drops. Rick *has* to do this to explain away the numerous inconsistencies in Q's ludicrous predictions. But the explanation brings up further problems. If you've acknowledged that Q knowingly spreads disinformation, why on Earth would you base every important decision in your life on what Q says?

Every other post could be a lie.

Every post could be a lie.

How would you ever know?

Fay Wray is DEAD.

Fay Wray is ALIVE.

Q is TRUTH.

Q is LIES.

★

During the first few hours after the insurrection, most people are quick to assume that the Trump supporters who broke into the Capitol are mere thugs and rednecks, lower-class clowns who forced their way into the building with no clear intent beyond stealing an envelope or lugging away Nancy Pelosi's podium or defecating and urinating in the halls.

As more and more firsthand details and video footage pours out from the Capitol, however, it becomes quite clear that among this surly mob of loutish fools were armed military men with a very clear, very serious intent.

What follows is a passage from Ronan Farrow's January 9, 2021 *New Yorker* article entitled "An Air Force Combat Veteran Breached the Senate":

> As insurrectionists stormed the U.S. Capitol this week, a few figures stood out. One man, clad in a combat helmet, body armor, and other tactical gear, was among the group that made it to the inner reaches of the building. Carrying zip-tie handcuffs, he was captured in photographs and videos on the Senate floor and with a group that descended on Speaker Nancy Pelosi's office suite. In a video shot by ITV News, he is seen standing against a wall adjacent to Pelosi's office, his face covered by a bandana. At another point, he appears to exit the suite, face exposed, pushing his way through the crowds of demonstrators.
>
> A day after the riots, John Scott-Railton, a senior researcher at Citizen Lab, at the University of Toronto's Munk School, notified the F.B.I. that he suspected the man was retired Lieutenant Colonel Larry Rendall Brock, Jr., a Texas-based Air Force Academy graduate and combat veteran [. . .].
>
> Brock denied that he had entered Pelosi's office suite, saying that he "stopped five to ten feet ahead of the sign" bearing her title that insurrectionists later tore down and brandished. However, in the ITV video, he appears to emerge from the suite. Brock said that he had worn tactical

gear because "I didn't want to get stabbed or hurt," citing "B.L.M. and Antifa" as potential aggressors. He claimed that he had found the zip-tie handcuffs on the floor. "I wish I had not picked those up," he told me. "My thought process there was I would pick them up and give them to an officer when I see one.... I didn't do that because I had put them in my coat, and I honestly forgot about them."[138]

[Insert sarcastic, incredulous comment here.—RG]

Now read this excerpt from Nick Visser's January 10, 2021 *Huffington Post* article entitled "FBI Arrests 2 Men Seen With Zip Tie Restraints During U.S. Capitol Riot":

Federal investigators arrested two men for entering the Senate chamber while carrying zip ties during the violent attack on the U.S. Capitol on Wednesday.

The FBI on Sunday said it arrested Eric Munchel, a 30-year-old from Nashville, Tennessee, who appeared to be the man photographed in military-style gear holding plastic restraints during the riot. Officials also arrested Larry Brock, who lives in Texas, saying he appeared to be holding "a white flex cuff, which is used by law enforcement to restrain and/or detain subjects."

The New York Times, citing officials involved in the case, said authorities recovered several weapons during Munchel's arrest. The FBI also said the photos of him appeared to show "an item in a holster on his right hip, and a cell phone mounted on his chest with the camera facing outward, ostensibly to record events that day."[139]

It should be obvious by now that these soldiers in Trump's army had a special mission that day: to truss up Nancy Pelosi, Mike Pence, and Chuck Schumer (and no doubt any other congressperson not onboard the Trump Train) and either hold them for hostage until their authoritarian demands were met or execute them on camera for the entire world to see, in full-on al Qaeda mode. If the insurrectionists had been able to breach the Senate floor only a few minutes earlier, this is undoubtedly what would have happened.

From Claire Lampen's January 10, 2021 article in *The Cut* entitled "Terrifying Details About the Capitol Hill Riots Keep Coming Out":

> The insurrectionists also constructed a gallows, complete with a noose, outside the Capitol—a detail that becomes all the more chilling in light of reports from witnesses who heard rioters calling for executions. Jim Bourg—Reuters News pictures editor in charge of Washington—says he "heard at least three different rioters at the Capitol say that they hoped to find Vice-President Mike Pence," and to hang "him from a Capitol Hill tree as a traitor."[140]

And the second these assassinations occurred, the President of the United States would have been justified in declaring marital law (for the safety of "The People," of course) and thus delaying the certification of Joe Biden as the President-elect.

Who had the means (the bully pulpit), the opportunity (he organized the protest), and the motive (preventing Biden's certification) to see this bloody scenario enacted?

Who lied to his followers for months about rampant election rigging?

Who branded his protest with the battle cry "STOP THE STEAL" (which sounds far more like a command than an appeal)?

Who delivered a fiery speech in which he pumped up a crowd of Q-heads with declarations to march on the Capitol, ordered them to "fight like hell," promised to stand beside them, wound them up like toy wooden soldiers, then hightailed it right back to the White House where he tweeted out further lies about what Mike Pence could do—constitutionally—to "STOP THE STEAL"?

Whose attorney screamed at the seething crowd, "Let's have trial by *combat!*" (like a far more nattily dressed version of one of the deranged marauders from *Escape from New York*)?

Whose loyal Republican colleague, Mo Brooks of Alabama, told the hordes that it was now time to "start taking down names and kicking ass"?

Whose convicted partner in crime, Roger Stone (the same jailbird who urged Trump back in September to "declare martial law" in case he lost the election[141]), addressed the masses the night before the insurrection to proselytize that they were fighting a holy war against the "godless" and the "evil"?

A well-educated elementary schooler, unclouded by ideology, shouldn't have any problem figuring out the basic answers to these basic questions.

Anyone who thinks it's impossible that Trump had full knowledge of what those "Zip Tie Guys" intended to do that day is not only dangerously naïve but lacking essential knowledge regarding the sordid history of military coups in Latin American countries (and elsewhere) from the end of World War II to the present day.

It should be painfully obvious by this point that the entire purpose of the QAnon narrative—a complex psychological warfare campaign intended to inculcate the American rightwing with not only a religious yearning for martial law but also a perverse hunger for an outright military coup in the U.S.—was a buildup to the insurrection of January 6 in case Trump lost what his 2016 campaign advisor Roger Stone characterized as "an already corrupt election."[142] Only a few quirks of fate prevented the plan from reaching full fruition. Unfortunately for Trump, his coup ended as successfully as the Bay of Pigs.

From Dan Koiss' January 8, 2021 *Slate* article entitled "They Were Out for Blood":

> They went into the Capitol, as Congress was counting electoral votes, equipped to take hostages—to physically seize officials, and presumably to take lives. The prospect is terrifying. But just because it seems unthinkable doesn't mean we shouldn't think hard about what almost happened. Don't dismiss the zip-tie guys as "LARPers" or "weekend warriors." First of all, given the well-documented overlap between ex-military, law enforcement, and right-wing militias, it's entirely possible these guys were weekday warriors using their training in service of extracurricular interests [. . .]. More importantly, the long awful course of history reminds us how slippery the slope is from playacting as a strike force to actually behaving as a strike force. Once the zip ties go on, it doesn't matter whether you're a "real" terrorist or not [. . .].
>
> But it could have been much, much worse. If the rioters had been a little quicker through the doors; if senators and representatives hadn't just moved from their joint session into separate chambers to debate the Arizona challenge and had instead still been packed into one harder-to-evacuate room; if any number of things had happened differently, the three people next in the line of succession for the presidency might have been face to face with those zip-tie guys. And then: Who knows.[143]

As with the Bay of Pigs, the people who orchestrated this blunder aren't going to just give up in passive despair. They almost succeeded once. Why not keep the chaos boiling and try again in the near future?

Maybe Trump won't even be involved in the scenario next time. It shouldn't be difficult to find another scarecrow to take his place. If you can convince thousands of full-grown adults to accept an oafish boor like Donald J. Trump as God's "Anointed One," you can get these rubes to accept almost anything or anyone.

As philosopher and Christian anarchist Jacques Ellul wrote in his 1965 book, *Propaganda: The Formation of Men's Attitudes*:

> [P]ropaganda offers release on a grand scale. For example, propaganda will permit what so far was prohibited, such as hatred, which is a dangerous and destructive feeling and fought by society. But man always has a certain need to hate, just as he hides in his heart the urge to kill. Propaganda offers him an object of hatred, for all propaganda is aimed at any enemy. And the hatred it offers him is not shameful, evil hatred that he must hide, but a legitimate hatred, which he can justly feel. Moreover, propaganda points out enemies that must be slain, transforming crime into a praiseworthy act. Almost every man feels a desire to kill his neighbor, but this is forbidden, and in most cases the individual will refrain from it for fear of the consequences. But propaganda opens the door and allows him to kill the Jews, the bourgeois, the Communists, and so on, and such murder even becomes an achievement [. . .]. In such cases the individual attaches himself passionately to the source of such propaganda, which, for him, provides liberation. Where transgression becomes virtue, the lifter of the ban becomes a hero, a demi-god, and we consecrate ourselves to serve him because he has liberated our repressed passions.[144]

For the past few years, the "lifter of the ban" has, of course, been Trump—and, by extension, Team QAnon.

The Great Liberators of Sublimated Hate.

The Great Awakening.

★

It's now January 12, 2021, and Rep. Mikie Sherill releases a video to her constituents in which she accuses fellow members of Congress of having aided and abetted the attack on the Capitol. Sherill and twenty-nine other House Democrats, according to a January 13 *Politico* article, are now "demanding information from Capitol security officials about 'suspicious' visitors at the U.S. Capitol [on the day before the attack] that would only have been permitted entry by a member of Congress . . ." The implication is that "some members of Congress may have provided 'reconnaissance' tours to would-be insurrectionists."[145]

Representatives Marjorie Taylor Greene of Georgia, Eric Berthel of Connecticut, Lauren Boebert of Colorado, and Madison Cawthorn of North Carolina (Republicans all) have made no secret of their allegiance to QAnon.

★

It's now January 16, and Gene decides to appear on a QAnon YouTube channel hosted by a woman named Cirsten Weldon. Weldon has a talent for spreading her own brand of QAnonense, including claims of assassination attempts against Trump that never occurred. Only recently, she insisted that:

> the 2018 false alarm about a missile threat in Hawaii was actually an assassination plot against Trump, and the red dots that appeared on Trump during the 2018 Christmas tree lighting

ceremony were part of a Mossad effort to "try to take him out." When Trump made a surprise and unexplained visit to a hospital in November 2019, Weldon claimed it was because Trump's official food taster was "in critical condition because they poisoned all the salt and all the water in the White House, so they had to pump his stomach."[146]

Now, just four days before Biden's inauguration, while obsessively primping her hair and gawking at herself in her Zoom camera, Weldon implores Gene to explain what *really* happened to Nancy Pelosi during the January 6 attack on the Capitol.

Here's Gene's response:

"The real Pelosi, during the first surrounding [of the Capitol], when she saw the National Guard, she went through the tunnels, went home, and then she ran for it down to the Gulf Coast of Florida, trying to get a deep sea fisherman guy to take her out past the military blockades. Then she went over to the Atlantic coastline and tried the same thing. She went all the way up to Myrtle Beach where she finally got somebody to take her out, but the guy was turned around by the Coast Guard. So then she went down to Charleston, and she went to the pier and a TR [Theodore Roosevelt, a nuclear aircraft carrier] asset came off the carrier and chased her down the street. Ridiculous! She's running down the street, goes into an alley with her bodyguard—her Chinese bodyguard, a Kung Fu guy—and they hid behind a dumpster. Like a TR isn't gonna see you behind a *dumpster*? So they captured her, and she's arrested.

"So the Pelosi we're seeing now is a clone. The submarine she was trying to get to was out past the blockade, and the carrier group scrambled assets, and they depth charged the bejeepers out of that thing [. . .]. The troops were sent in, and all the people in the Congress and Senate have already been cited to be under arrest, and the secret Space Program fleet that Trump has—they have technology that can render people unconscious, and they just go in, make 'em all go to sleep, and pick 'em all up.

"So Trump signed the Insurrection Act, and all he has to do is announce it. It's a classified document. It can't be shown to the public. The people who are saying that it's not signed don't understand the law. It's signed, but until he announces it publically, and then shows it at the same time, it's not active. It'll be active once he shows it in public.

"We're in a very high state of alert. There're military troops all over the country. The National Guard's activated."

In case you're having trouble following all of that, here's a summation: The National Guard has been deployed not because a mob of violent QAnon followers assaulted the Capitol, but because Nancy Pelosi and her Kung Fu bodyguard attempted to escape the secret Space Program fleet inside a foreign submarine.

With a straight face, Weldon then says, "I have a question for you. Do you think they're going to let the Biden inauguration go on?"

Gene: "From what I've been told, the plan is that they'll let it start, then they'll announce the Insurrection Act and arrest Biden in the process. That's currently what the plan is."[147]

★

It's now the Big Day: January 20, 2021. The Moment of Truth.

Rick is wearing a black t-shirt that features the words "TRUST THE PLAN" in red, white, and blue. This slogan is superimposed over an immense cross.

Rick begins his show by saying, "There's a cross on this t-shirt for a reason [. . .]. 'Cause this is *not* Trump's plan or Q's plan. It *is* God's plan. And obviously God is deciding that He needs to wake more people up. [Laughs] It's clear that that's exactly what's happening here! And we're gonna go into why *we're* still winning! We're winning every day in a big way because we have military operations all over the world. It's not just the U.S. military. A lot of other militaries are participating and have signed up in this movement to take this Cabal down. The Cabal *is* going down! Now it's just the matter of the timing and how many darn Americans we have to wake up! [. . .] I want people to focus on the right things here. Remember: Falling into fear creates a lack of faith. If you continue having faith, you're one of the remnants, one of the red-pilled Patriots. You're part of the *Army*! If you think [. . .] Amanda Grace is a false prophet, everything that Q's done is false, then that would mean that . . ." Rick's voice falters. The next thought that crosses Rick's mind is clearly disturbing to him. "Because Q Proofs show that clearly Trump and Q are like *this*." He links his hands together. "You'd have to believe that *Trump* is false." He shakes his head darkly. "That's not goin' on . . . right? That means if you believe in Trump, if you believe in Jesus [points up at the ceiling of his little studio], and most importantly, if you believe in the Lord God Almighty, the Lord of the Universe, you need to *hold* the line. And everybody who's a red-pilled Christian Patriot needs to be a part of that because there're people falling out of line right and left right now, as if the world's over. And it's not. We're seeing Joe [Biden] display what *would* happen if we gave him four years. He would destroy this country. But he's not gonna get four years [. . .] I think we have to get to some of these middle-of-the-road Democrats, as well as some of these Trump supporters who've given up, wake them up to how bad this would be. And I think it's all coming, guys, it's all coming [. . .]. This is a place to come to for optimism, hope, and *truth*. I pray that only truth prevails on this channel!"

Gene then comes on the show to reveal THE MOST STARTLING TRUTH OF ALL! You see, it's "a fairly decent probability" that on March 4, 2021, Biden will be removed from the White House by the U.S. military and Trump will be placed back in power. "That's the most likely probability at this time," Gene insists. "We're in a jumbled timeline where the moves and countermoves of the Cabal and the Alliance are what decides what things happen."

Rick shakes his head and replies, "Wow. What a shame that we have to give power to the criminals for a while to show everybody how horrible of an administration it would've been… if we left it alone."

In response to all the evil Democrats who are laughing at those who have placed their faith in Q for the past few years, Gene has this response: "They were laughing at Noah right up until it started pouring rain. Building a big, huge boat in the middle of the land, and putting on animals and all kinds of stuff? For those who doubt it, look at the side of Mount Ararat at 13,000-plus feet and it sits there today. That's how high the water got! So go ahead and let your friends laugh at you . . . until it starts pourin' rain on the Cabal again!"[148]

This video has received 20,947 views within six hours of being posted on YouTube.

★

It's now March 4, the day the U.S. military is scheduled to barge into the Oval Office, drag Biden out by the hair, and replace him with Trump at long last.

Needless to say, this doesn't happen.

So Rick begins today's episode by telling his loyal flock, "Make sure you're not watching the news before you're in the Word of God because Satan's using that to try to control you into his timeline [. . .]. It's kind of like a virus, *affecting* you!"

After this wise advice, Gene appears on the show to announce that two hundred members of the Special Forces lost their lives earlier that day while liberating a Cabal-controlled military base located deep beneath the Atlantic Ocean. Not a single mention is made of the fact that Gene's prediction about March 4 has not come to pass. His previous statement ("That's the most likely probability at this time") warrants at least a passing mention of the date, does it not?

Rick and Gene aren't even bothering to explain the discrepancies anymore.

Instead, Gene informs his audience that the World Wildlife Fund—the largest conservation organization on Earth—*must* be defunded as soon as possible. Why? The symbol of the WWF is a panda and has been since the organization's establishment in 1961.

Here's a direct quote from Gene: "The panda logo is a well-known pedophile symbol."

Rick nods, then says, "Mm-hm. Yeah, wow. Very sick."[149]

"Very sick" is an appropriate diagnosis, of course.

But not for the panda.

★

It's now March 23, and Sidney Powell has concocted a rather peculiar defense in response to the fact that Dominion Voting Systems is suing her for claiming repeatedly that the company's voting machines rigged the 2020 election in favor of Joe Biden.

Here's a passage from Katelyn Polantz's March 23, 2021 CNN report entitled "Sidney Powell Argues in New Court

Filing That No Reasonable People Would Believe Her Election Fraud Claims":

> Right-wing lawyer Sidney Powell is claiming in a new court filing that reasonable people wouldn't have believed as fact her assertions of fraud after the 2020 presidential election.
>
> The election infrastructure company Dominion Voting Systems sued Powell for defamation after she pushed lawsuits and made appearances in conservative media on behalf of then-President Donald Trump to sow doubt about the 2020 election results. Dominion claims that Powell knew her election fraud accusations were false and hurtful to the company.
>
> In a new court filing, Powell's attorneys write that she was sharing her "opinion" and that the public could reach "their own conclusions" about whether votes were changed by election machines.
>
> "Given the highly charged and political context of the statements, it is clear that Powell was describing the facts on which she based the lawsuits she filed in support of President Trump," Powell's defense lawyers wrote in a court filing on Monday.
>
> "Indeed, Plaintiffs themselves characterize the statements at issue as 'wild accusations' and 'outlandish claims.' They are repeatedly labelled 'inherently improbable' and even 'impossible.' Such characterizations of the allegedly defamatory statements further support Defendants' position that reasonable people would not accept such statements as fact but view them only as claims that await testing by the courts through the adversary process."[150]

Translation: The obvious fact that Powell's assertions are 100 percent bullshit is the exact same reason she shouldn't be held liable for uttering them over and over again in public. After all (say Powell and her lawyers), what kind of a halfwit would allow themselves to believe such nonsense? Certainly no one of any real consequence . . .

★

It's now March 24, and Rick is hosting his first episode since Sidney Powell and her attorneys threw him, Gene, and the entire B2T audience under the bus by essentially describing them as unreasonable naifs. During this hour-plus episode, Rick never utters a single word about Powell's damning statement. If Rick follows the news at all, he couldn't have missed hearing about the Powell story, which was plastered all over the internet the previous day. Perhaps we shouldn't be surprised by Rick's silence on this matter. After all, as Rick himself said, "Make sure you're not watching the news before you're in the Word of God because Satan's using that to try to control you . . ." Instead of acknowledging reality, Rick chooses to sink deeper into fantasy and begins pushing the notion that Trump will be "back in office by August."

At one point, Rick says that he and his followers need to abandon mainstream conservatives who are already strategizing for the next Presidential election in 2024. "Where we need to be fighting is with General Flynn and Sidney Powell!" Rich says. "We need to be fighting with Lin Wood [an attorney who publicly backed Trump's allegations that vote rigging cost him a second term]. These are the people we need to be fighting with [. . .]. I'm personally not going to be messing with people who're talking about 2024. Again, that's why all my t-shirts that are coming out pretty soon are going to say, 'TRUMP 2021!' *All* my 2020 t-shirts are changing to '2021' because I think that's when it's gonna happen! That might not be as early as you want it, but it *will* happen . . . and in an amazing way."[151]

★

It's now April 20 (Hitler's 132nd birthday), and numerous articles have begun to appear in various mainstream publications that attempt to lay the blame/credit for the entire QAnon phenomenon on a single person: Ron Watkins, the administrator of the 8kun message board.[152] Most of these articles were inspired by Cullen Hoback's recent HBO documentary, *Q: Into the Storm*, which is hardly definitive in proving its central thesis. Hoback's attempts to pin the job on Watkins are based on little more than circumstantial evidence, innuendo, and rumor—the same logically fallacious pitfalls upon which the QAnon narrative has been constructed from the very beginning.

If Watkins was indeed *solely* responsible for QAnon, I have some key questions for him: "Ron, are you the one who directed Maj. Gen. Paul E. Vallely—a highly decorated military figure in the U.S. Army—to appear on a Canadian radio show just a few months before the lockdown for the express purpose of conning thousands of listeners into believing that Q is a real intelligence officer who's been feeding 'very valid' information to the President of the United States?[153] If so, how did you go about contacting Maj. Gen. Vallely? Did you know each other socially? Did you two like-minded patriots just happen to hook up randomly in a 4chan chatroom? And if *you* didn't contact Maj. Gen. Vallely, who did? Or did Vallely simply volunteer to come out of retirement and blatantly lie to the entire world for no particular reason, merely for shits 'n giggles?" It should be obvious that a high-ranking military officer like Maj. Gen. Paul E. Vallely doesn't take his marching orders from a creep like Ron Watkins.

Though Hoback is hyperfocused on uncovering the exact identity of Q, I would argue that this is not the most fascinating aspect of the QAnon phenomenon. Anonymous people have been posting convoluted, baseless conspiracy theories online since the inception of the internet. Not only would most people have trouble keeping track of all of these theories, under normal circumstances they wouldn't even be interested in doing so. The most important question is: What is it about QAnon that attracted so many average people? What is it about QAnon that attracted so many *educated* Americans? Americans like the Arizona college professor who was fired for teaching his English students that JFK, Jr. is still alive and eager to join Trump in an all-out war against Satanism.[154] Americans like the Florida middle school teacher who told her students that Antifa covertly led the charge against the Capitol Building on January 6.[155] Americans like the Chapman University constitutional law scholar who addressed the crowd at Trump's "Save America" rally and spoke about the existence of "'secret folders' in ballot machines that were used to skew vote totals" and "questioned [Kamala] Harris' birthright citizenship and eligibility to become vice president."[156] It might be comforting to think that only the most extreme initiates of the uneducated, basement-dwelling "Proud Boy" contingency became ensnared in Q's web, but that's clearly not the case. The siren call of Q extended far beyond The Three Percenters, The Oath Keepers, and Texas Freedom Force. Perhaps the most intriguing aspect of the QAnon psyop is not the identity of its architects, but the mere fact that it *worked* . . . and worked so damn well.

★

It's now June 27, and *Business Insider* is reporting that thirty-six congressional candidates running in the 2022 midterm elections have "either openly endorsed QAnon, made subtle references to, or distanced themselves from the conspiracy theory despite repeatedly displaying their support on social media or in video interviews. Thirty-three of the candidates are running as Republicans while two are independents and one is still deciding whether to run as a Republican or an independent."[157]

The article goes on to profile several of these candidates. Perhaps one of the most peculiar is Omar Navarro, a resident of my hometown of Torrance, California. Navarro was arrested in San Francisco in 2019 for stalking his ex-girlfriend, a Republican politician named DeAnna Lorraine Tesoriero who unsuccessfully ran a campaign against Nancy Pelosi in 2020.[158] This is the same Tesoriero who said that George Floyd's family must have been offered "free meth" to attend the Democratic National Convention.[159] Clearly, she and Navarro must have made quite a pair at one time. Navarro pled guilty to the stalking charge and spent six months in a San Francisco jail, but incarceration did not curb Navarro's political ambitions. In January of 2021, he announced he would be running for California's forty-third congressional district for the fourth time.

Here are two excerpts from the *Business Insider* report:

The California native [. . .] told *Insider* in an interview that he believes in "some things" that "Q" says, including the human trafficking trope.

"I do believe that there's human trafficking going on right now. I do believe that Hollywood has participated in some of this with pedophilia and it's something obviously we can't ignore," he said.

Navarro, who has gone viral multiple times on Twitter for his far-right and homophobic views, has previously pushed the debunked Pizzagate theory. He told *Insider*: "I feel like there are certain things going on. There's something shady in that pizza shop [. . .]."

It's clear that the influence of QAnon in congressional politics is "on the rise," [*Media Matters* president Angelo] Carusone said. "And they're aggressively moving to take over parts of the Republican party, local committees, school boards, local races too."

[Rutgers University professor Jack] Bratich said it shows how deeply QAnon has "settled" into the Republican party. "As a movement, it has expanded to try and take over the party," he said. "It's not central to the GOP but it's no longer a marginal component either."

QAnon is now a major force in American politics, Carusone agreed. "And, basically, I think we're kind of screwed."[160]

★

It's now July 4, and MyPillow CEO Mike Lindell assures the listeners of the conservative WVW Broadcast Network that Donald Trump will be reinstated as President on the 13th of August. His exact words: "The morning of August 13, it'll be the talk of the world, going, 'Hurry up! Let's get this election pulled down, let's right the right, let's get these communists out, you know, that have taken over!'"[161]

Due to Lindell's continued false claims that Trump won the 2020 election, companies like Bed Bath & Beyond, Costco, Kohl's, H-E-B, and Wayfair decide to stop carrying MyPillow products in their stores.[162]

Our old friend, Rick Rene, demonstrates his support of Lindell and his predictions by offering MyPillow products through his website at extreme discounts. At the beginning of his show, right after airing an ad for a Christian t-shirt that reads "Instead of 'Be Less White' 'Be More Like Jesus'" (the preceding dictum is printed on the t-shirt in white letters against a red background, mimicking the Coca-Cola logo), Rick emblazons the following ad across his screen:

★

It's now August 11, and multiple news sources are reporting the tragic murder of a young brother and sister, ages ten months and two years old. The culprit? Their father, a QAnon devotee who used a speargun to impale both children, and then dumped their bodies in a ditch in Mexico. Journalist Jean Yamamura of *The Santa Barbara Independent* writes:

> Santa Barbara resident Matthew Taylor Coleman, 40, was charged today by the U.S. Attorney's Office in Los Angeles for the crimes of murdering his two young children on foreign soil. According to an affidavit by an FBI Special Agent, he confessed to the murders of his two children [. . .] during an interview, allegedly stating he believed they "were going to grow into monsters." Coleman is the owner of Lovewater Surf School in Santa Barbara.
>
> According to the FBI affidavit, during Coleman's confession, "M. Coleman stated that he believed his children were going to grow into monsters so he had to kill them." The affidavit further states Coleman said "he was enlightened by QAnon and Illuminati conspiracy theories and was receiving

visions and signs" that his wife had passed "serpent DNA" to their children. When asked if he knew what he did was wrong, Coleman acknowledged it was, but he had to save the world.

The FBI investigation so far has involved the Santa Barbara Police Department and the County District Attorney's Office. Coleman's wife had reported to Santa Barbara Police on Saturday, August 7, that her husband had taken their little boy and infant daughter in their Sprinter van, though she had expected them all to go camping. She met with an officer the next day after her attempts to reach Coleman by phone, along with attempts by other family members, went unanswered. She stated they'd had no problems or arguments, and she didn't believe they were in danger.[163]

Further details about Coleman are revealed in Jamie Ross and Justin Rohrlich's August 11, 2021 *Daily Beast* article entitled "Surf School Owner Killed Kids After Being 'Enlightened' by QAnon":

Lovewater Surf School's website shows several photos of the Coleman family together. Coleman's biography states that he taught high school for several years before founding the surf school.

The surf instructor posted about his Christian faith online, wondering in a November 2020 Facebook post whether "there is a type of Great American Renaissance following the years of Covid, censorship, and political divisiveness. . . that will empower each person's heart to come alive and explode with innovative ideas, new business models, new music sounds and never seen ways to build an amazing community?"

Just a month earlier, Coleman had celebrated the birth of the couple's youngest child, Roxy Rain, in an Instagram post.

"While waiting for her to come, I kept feeling this sense that she was going to be born at a very pivotal time in history and that she would represent a dawn, or even awakening, to years of great blessing for our family and nation," he wrote. "Another picture that came to me was of God reaching down into a river bed and picking up a small stone (rock), examining it intently. Just as David had done before slaying Goliath, God examined the stone and was confident that it was just the perfect one for the battle. Although it was small, smooth and somewhat harmless looking, he knew that it would become great when placed into the palm of a skilled hand. My declaration over Roxy Rain is that she has been hand picked by God to slay the giants in the land."[164]

Save the children, indeed.

★

It's now August 13, and Donald Trump can be found nowhere near the *Resolute* desk or any other item of furniture in the Oval Office. Nonetheless, Jenni Fink of *Newsweek* reports that one in ten registered voters refuse to relinquish their belief that Trump will be back in power by the end of 2021:

> With a margin of error of two percent, the number of Republicans who believe it's "very likely" Trump will return to office has remained essentially unchanged. In June, seventeen percent thought it was "very likely," and that number was at sixteen percent on Wednesday's poll. The Morning Consult/ Politico survey found eleven percent of all registered voters believe Trump will be reinstated by the end of the year.[165]

★

It's now August 16, the first time Rick has produced a new episode since the non-event of August 13, and true to form no mention is made of Trump's failure to regain the White House; however, we do learn the "real" reason behind the Taliban's recent return to power in Afghanistan:

"I believe the white hats are allowing [the Taliban to take over Afghanistan] for a period of time, but maybe there's a better way of saying it. Maybe God's allowing this to happen to wake up many people. He's about ready to have the most awesome show on Earth! He is going to show off in an amazing way, and *we* get to be a part of that. I believe it's going to happen here in the next few months. It's going to be something we're not expecting, I believe. But it's going to flip around this whole script, and the Cabal is going to be exposed like never before. And they *are* being exposed—in layers. Different layers of people are waking up all the time. More and more people are waking up as this *'America Last'* movie [. . .] is playing right before us: Communists first, China first, coming right before our eyes. And we *had* to see this! This is part of what 16+1 [Rick's code word for Q] was saying: 'Hey, sometimes you have to show people because you can't *tell* them.' You can't tell them what's going to happen. Now we're *showing* them. Look what happened in Afghanistan. Look what happened to our border. Look what happened with communism coming in. Look what happened with Critical Race Theory coming in. This is what happens when you have machines that control who goes in [the White House], right? [. . .]"

"We're showing weakness and wokeness. *Wokeness is what the apple offered to Eve!* The forbidden fruit that was offered to Eve was . . . what? What was it? 'Hey, you'll open up your eyes! You'll be *woke*! You eat of the forbidden fruit and you will see evil—like the *Lord*.' It was a big *deception*. So you can be deceived too. 'Become woke!' Just like Eve was woke after she took the apple. Interesting parallels [. . .]."

"World-wide, there's a huge push. Satan wants [the COVID vaccine] to be completely mandatory. That is the big push they are trying to tackle, to lockdown everything and get to the Great Reset. That is [Satan's] chance to change the timeline, to get into all levels of *Revelation* as soon as possible. God's already denied that timeline. You're gonna see a huge reversal here as more and more people *wake up*."[166]

Only a few minutes earlier, Rick warned his flock about never buying into any ideology that claimed people needed to "wake up" (and/or become "woke"), comparing such modes of thinking to Eve being tricked by Lucifer into believing that she needed to "wake up" from her Gnostic prison, and yet repeatedly—several times during a single episode, in fact—Rick will insist that the main purpose of Q's teachings is to "wake" the sheeple out of their slumber. Why is this sleeping/awake metaphor comparable to the temptations of a fallen angel one minute and yet employed by Rick as a rhetorical tool only moments later? What's Rick really trying to tell us here? Is it possible that Rick is far closer to the truth than even *he* knows? Doesn't the Bible tell us that Satan often quotes Scripture to get his way?

In the tangled, overgrown garden of the internet, snakes can manifest in a multiplicity of guises. Some can even appear as letters of the alphabet.

Others pretend to be dead American writers.

★

It's now August 21, and I (or rather Edgar Allan Poe) receive an urgent email entitled "NEW THREAT." It's from Rick.

Hey Ed,

Let's face it: If you're like me, you probably suspect the "Big Shot" is dangerous . . .

I never thought it could be this dangerous.

Turns out, the "Big Shot" is 500x more dangerous than every vaccine in the past 30 years combined . . .

It's true. That's what the U.S. Centers for Disease Control recently published.

Worst [sic] still, new evidence has come to light that it's not only dangerous . . .

It can spread from person to person – through saliva, skin flakes or even mucus.

I don't know about you, but that means I want to take action to enhance my natural immune system!

Why?

Because whether or not you plan to get the vaccine . . . you could still be at risk.

Luckily, there is a simple way to help protect yourself from this contagious threat - without needing medicine or doctors.

Click here here to find out how to supercharge your immunity without drugs

God Bless,

Rick B2T

Who could pass up such an offer? "Not I!" says I, clicking on the link and immediately discovering the wonders of the "QUANTUM ENERGY IMMUNE BOOST SKIN PATCH." This lightweight, portable, handy-dandy patch is encoded with Biblical scriptures that help "bring your frequencies into balance."

Yes, my friend, you heard me right. According to the ad: "There Are Over 40 Scriptural Frequencies Taken Directly From The Bible Encoded Onto Every Quantum Energy

Immune Boost Skin Patch!" Please continue reading to see just a few of the miraculous Words of Power with which these wondrous patches are encoded:

> "**But thou, O LORD, art a shield for me.** My glory, and the lifter up of mine head. I cried unto the LORD with my voice, and he heard me out of his holy hill. Selah. I laid me down and slept; I awaked; for the LORD sustained me." (Psalm 3:3-5)
>
> "**The Spirit of Life is making your body alive.** But if the Spirit of Him who raised Jesus from the dead dwells in you, He who raised Christ from the dead will also give life to your mortal bodies through His Spirit who dwells in you." (Rom 8:11)
>
> "**One of God's benefits is healing.** Bless the LORD, O my soul; And all that is within me, bless His holy name. Bless the LORD, O my soul, And forget not all His benefits: Who forgives all your iniquities, Who heals all your diseases, Who redeems your life from destruction, Who crowns you with loving kindness and tender mercies, Who satisfies your mouth with good things, So that your youth is renewed like the eagle's." (Psalm 103:1-5)

Translation: You needn't bother with some dumb, nasty, new-fangled vaccine when you can boost your immune system naturally by applying to your bicep a thin, circular piece of paper with microscopic Bible verses printed on its adhesive surface. As the ad itself proclaims, "Every substance from the largest object (even the Earth) down to the smallest subatomic particle vibrates at a specific frequency (speed of vibration). Many scientists and researchers have concluded that these frequencies are the glue holding our Universe together. They believe these omnipresent vibrations came from the word of God as He spoke creation into existence."

You see? The Creator's holy words *themselves* can heal any illness, including COVID-19, if attached to one's flesh like a NicoDerm cigarette patch. Why do you look so gobsmacked? This is merely a logical extension of the sigil magic Grant Morrison and Douglas Rushkoff discussed earlier. After all, what's good enough for any progressive coven of witches or warlocks in Hollywood should be good enough for this New Breed of righteous patriots who now understand that the most sinful aspect of the Thelemic magick developed by Aleister Crowley back in the 1920s is that it wasn't being exploited by the followers of Jesus.

A 3x7 pack of Biblical Skin Sigils costs only $21.98. The shipping is free, and you have a 100% money back guarantee for a full sixty days. What're you waiting for? Why not give them a chance? What do you have to lose?

★

It's now September 3, and National Public Radio is reporting that Jake Chansley (AKA Jake Angeli, the aforementioned "QAnon Shaman" who, while clothed in animal furs, helped lead the mob of Trump supporters into the Capitol building on January 6) has pled guilty to a felony charge for his role in the insurrection:

> Jacob Chansley, who was widely photographed in the Senate chamber with a flagpole topped with a spear, could face 41 to 51 months in prison under sentencing guidelines, a prosecutor said. The man who called himself "QAnon Shaman" has been jailed for nearly eight months since his arrest.
>
> Before entering the plea, Chansley was found by a judge to be mentally competent after having been transferred to a Colorado facility for a mental health evaluation [. . .].

Chansley's lawyer said his client has since repudiated the QAnon movement and asked that there be no more references to his past affiliations with the movement.[167]

★

It's worth noting that not all of QAnon's early "fans" were completely taken in by the scam. After the first part of my QAnon series was published by *Salon*, I received an email from an associate who participated live in the very first Q post when it popped up out of nowhere on 4chan in October of 2017. In retrospect, he had this to say about the experience:

I've been front row for Q since day 1. The first Q post was a series of questions posted by someone claiming to be an insider. The gist was that we now finally have an insider at the highest levels, letting us know that for the first time, someone was actually going to take a run at the ruling class (deep state). I can't recall with perfect certainty, but among the couple things this first Q post mentioned was that Michael Flynn was a victim of a coup attempt, and that we should trust that there are people in Trump's inner circle who are aware of this, and that we needed to be patient as they needed to navigate this extremely carefully and quietly if anything was to ever come of it . . . none of the more fantastical demon pedophile stuff was part of Q in the beginning, beyond some pretty anodyne stuff about trust in god/the truth shall reveal . . .

Anyway, what gave this LARP some legs was that someone started posting pics from clearly inside the white house. It was early in xmas season, and I think it was the day (or day after) they started putting up xmas decorations around the white house, and someone was posting pics of the decorations, which we were able to correlate to official images of the white house xmas. someone was clearly there snapping pics and, on 4chan, since everybody is lying and larping all the time, the custom is to post proof by timestamping the pics. So, for example, people will write down the day's date, the time, and "/pol//" and include it in the photo. When people challenged the person posting the pics, more pics were posted with various forms of timestamps. It was pretty clear that there was at least one person physically in the white house at least for this moment who read or was somewhat familiar with /pol/ and /pol/ culture. Of course, it could have been an elaborate ruse (never put anything past internet nerds), but the board seemed to generally accept the pics poster as legit, acceptance that is not easily won nor freely given around those parts.

Note that the xmas pics thing happened in a separate thread later that day or the next day, NOT in the original Q post. The xmas pics person was not Q and never claimed to be Q, BUT the xmas pics poster did tell us that Q was legit. But it wasn't an explicit confirmation. It was more like, yes, there are now people on the inside who will challenge the old ruling order, that there are people within Trump/Bannon's orbit who do want to actually make changes in Washington, and that the original Q post seemed to be at least correctly familiar with what was going on in that particular scene. So, this gave us all a whiff that there was something of substance here beyond typical 4chan shenanigans.

From there, it took off like wildfire. It was a perfect storm sort of thing, triggering a lot of confirmation bias, etc. Q posts started coming in non-stop. And, of course, they quickly became more and more insane. And, the way 4chan works, nobody actually knows if any subsequent Q posts were written by the original Q. Some tried to imitate the style/voice of the original, and many were clearly just people goofing around. It's very possible that the original Q never posted again ever. Suddenly, everybody was Q. They called it Q-posting. It was just a giddy sort of fun. Also, part of the culture of /pol/ is to say and "prove" the most outlandish possible things - the more ridiculous the claim, and the more flimsy and circumstantial the "evidence," the better. And when some hapless goof would come along and try to push back against the veracity of our claims, we would double and triple and quadruple down. That was the game. To this day, one of my friend groups constantly jokes about adrenochrome, the more outlandish the better. Are you aware that fear improves the purity and potency of adrenochrome production? That's why the missing kids are tortured and raped and kept alive in underground facilities. . . .

This was all fun and games while it was contained on /pol/. The problem is that 4chan, and ESPECIALLY /pol/, culture is near impenetrable to outsiders. It's so many inside jokes and layers of irony and tongue-in-cheek. Normal people living normal lives are just not mentally equipped to even begin to comprehend this stuff. . . .

Is there another example of a big conspiracy theory that started as an inside joke?

The answer: Yes. In fact, I covered this in Chapter One of my first book, *Cryptoscatology: Conspiracy Theory as Art Form* (2012). *The Protocols of the Learned Elders of Zion* (one of the main texts used by the Nazis to justify the Holocaust) began as a satire entitled *Dialogue in Hell Between Machiavelli and Montesquieu*, which was written by Maurice Joly and published in France in 1865. If you want to read a clear, concise account of how Joly's work was hijacked by the Nazis and transformed into one of the most effective propaganda tools in modern history, I highly recommend Will Eisner's 2006 nonfiction graphic novel, *The Plot: The Secret Story of The Protocols of the Elders of Zion*.

Léo Taxil's *Les mystères de la Franc-Maçonnerie dévoilés,* which was published in France a couple of decades after Joly's book, attributed all kinds of outrageously lurid and supernaturally tinged sex crimes to the Freemasons. Taxil intended the book to be a satire on the extreme paranoia running rampant among devout Catholics regarding any "unorthodox" group not affiliated with the Roman Catholic Church.

More recently, in the latter half of the twentieth century, we have the case of Lewis Lewin's *Report From Iron Mountain* (1967), which satirized the extremes to which the U.S. government might go to keep the war machine churning even during times of peace. In the book, a fictional government task force called "Iron Mountain 15" dreams up various methods of "invisible warfare" in order to keep the economy on an even keel, including staging terrorist attacks on U.S. soil and elaborately faking invasions from outer space.

Of course, it's possible that the QAnon phenomenon began as satire as well. If so, somebody very quickly realized how useful this "joke" could be and decided to exploit it as a readymade propaganda tool. It's also possible that QAnon was generated from the very beginning as a means to divide the country, sow seeds of fear and paranoia among the populace, and propel Trump back into the White House. If the latter function was its central goal, it did not succeed; however, one should be concerned about how *very close* it came to doing precisely that.

Here's an excerpt from a November 10, 2020 *Washington Post* article by Drew Harwell and Craig Timburg:

> Rita Katz, the executive director of SITE Intelligence Group, which monitors online extremism, said she expects the QAnon following will continue to grow online, regardless of who created or operated its presence online.
>
> "It's a dangerous network. It's a dangerous movement that truly believes that Biden and other Democrats are killing kids," Katz said. "And now, with Biden's projected victory, the QAnon movement believes with the same zealous certainty that the whole thing is a sham. And that's a major problem, because... these aren't a bunch of harmless keyboard warriors—they're adherents of a movement that has resulted in real-life violence."

The FBI said last year that QAnon and other "conspiracy theory-driven domestic extremists" represented a major terrorism threat. Its supporters have been linked to kidnapping plots and violent threats, including in 2018, when an armed man in Arizona barricaded a bridge at the Hoover Dam with an armored truck.

QAnon followers have more recently pushed one another to keep the faith. On the far-right message board Gab, one user reposted a Q drop from June: "These are the times that try men's souls."

For some core QAnon believers, who call themselves "digital soldiers," the election seemed to fuel new calls for violent action in the real world.

"WAR," one QAnon account wrote shortly after the race had been called on Saturday, in a tweet that has been retweeted more than 1,000 times. "Patriots will handle from here," it read, alongside a "storm" emoji.[168]

The cognitive dissonance among the QAnon crowd has never been more pronounced than right now. Given the extreme state of denial in which these people have placed themselves, I would not have been at all surprised if, at the moment Joe Biden placed his hand on the Bible and was sworn in as the forty-sixth President of the United States, willfully blind followers like Rick Rene would take to the internet and insist, "Don't believe the fake news, my friends! That's not Sleepy Joe! No! That's just a *hologram*! It's really Trump in disguise! He's been planning this all along! He's succeeded in fooling the Deep State at last! We win! We *win*!"

Despite the fact that Biden has now been sworn in as President, I suspect Trump and his most ardent followers aren't going anywhere anytime soon. Obviously, Trump has left the White House. . . but he's not going to leave the spotlight. Thousands of U.S. citizens are convinced that Trump is the real President of the United States. I can see it now: Trump moving out of the U.S., launching his own streaming channel, and trying to govern his acolytes from some "shithole country" via Zoom, just another in a long line of would-be dictators forced to flee his country of origin in the middle of the night after a bungled coup attempt. No, the "Fake News" Era isn't quite over yet.

So what's the answer to this precarious situation? Is it to "deplatform" all of Trump's followers on Twitter and Facebook and YouTube? I doubt such an authoritarian move will solve anything. When has suppressing anyone's point of view, whether inaccurate or not, solved *any* problem?

In the words of Kate Ruane, a senior legislative counsel at the ACLU:

> For months, President Trump has been using social media platforms to seed doubt about the results of the election and to undermine the will of voters. We understand the desire to permanently suspend him now, but it should concern everyone when companies like Facebook and Twitter wield the unchecked power to remove people from platforms that have become indispensable for the speech of billions—especially when political realities make those decisions easier. President Trump can turn to his press team or Fox News to communicate with the public, but others—like many Black, Brown, and LGTBQ activists who have been censored by social media companies—will not have that luxury. It is our hope that these companies will apply their rules transparently to everyone.[169]

Ask yourself: When has suppression ever resulted in the weakening of *any* movement? Can you name a time when slamming a boot down on an idea didn't end up making that idea even more resilient? At what time in history have religious fanatics *not* loved martyrs? Suppression only makes the extremists even more convinced that their point of view is the correct one. "Otherwise, how come the Democrat-controlled media's trying so hard to crack down on us?!" "Rick B2T" is saying exactly those words on his podcast even as I write this. It surprises me, perhaps more so recently, when otherwise rational adults—supporters of the First Amendment in almost all other circumstances—refuse to see the inevitable result of censorious stratagems like this.

In fact, it causes me to wonder if someone, somewhere, doesn't have a vested interest in making certain that the flames of extremism don't die out in America quite so quickly. After all, why let an angry mob filled with unthinking extremists go to waste?

The most workable solution, of course, is to push back against lies with truth. Despite the seemingly impenetrable madness of QAnon, the cracks in the psyop are growing wider by the second.

As one QAnon proponent wrote on 8kun, not long after Election Day, "HOW CAN I SPEAK TO Q???? MY FAITH IS SHAKEN. I FOLLOWED THE PLAN. TRUMP LOST!!!!!!!!!!! WHAT NOW?????? WHERE IS THE PLAN???"[170]

Sorry, my friend. "THE PLAN" has run out of funds. Team QAnon has moved on to other assignments. You need to power this live action roleplaying game on your own steam now. Someone needs to step up and take the reins, right? It might as well be you. Wrack your brains. Think about it. What other innocent people can you stalk and harass online, then in the real world, with baseless accusations while telling yourself you're doing it all for Mom, God, and Apple Pie? The Earth has no shortage of vulnerable targets. Just go looking for one or two or three. You'll be sure to find them.

As long as the potential targets far outnumber the larping stalkers, your chosen profession will be secure for the foreseeable future.

No matter *which* scarecrow occupies the White House.

★

"After the violent attack on the U.S. Capitol, 139 Republican members of the House and eight members of the Senate, led by Sens. Josh Hawley and Ted Cruz, came out of hiding to vote to object to the electoral college vote count. While a police officer lay dying, they supported Trump's lie of a stolen election and embraced the insurrectionists' cause.

"Imagine the events of the past weeks and months if some-one like Hawley had been the secretary of state in Georgia, or someone like retired Lt. Gen. Michael Flynn held a significant military command. Imagine what would have happened if the Republicans held majorities in both houses of Congress and could have overturned the electoral college results. Imagine if the courts had been more generously stocked with judges willing to entertain the Trump campaign's ludicrous arguments.

"Above all, imagine if the president had been a bit more competent, a bit more strategic, a bit more daring. Hitler, after all, was at least willing to be present at the violence his words inspired. He was also more persuasive in his dealings with important officials.

"It is much more common for democracies to be undermined by seemingly legal actions taken from within than by violence from without."

—Benjamin Carter Hett, *Los Angeles Times*, "The Trump Insurrection Was America's Beer Hall Putsch," 1-16-21

Acknowledgments

Special thanks to Rod Barroso, Eric Blair, Catherine Bottolfson McCallum, Mason Boyer, Joe Brown, Steve Cooper, Chris Doyle, Melissa Guffey, Olivia Guffey, Eric A. Johnson, Randy Koppang, Clint Margrave, Alan Moore, John Oakes, George Porcari, Adam Sayne, Steve Snider, Serfeil Stevenson, Jack Womack, and Ray Zepeda for their valuable assistance and encouragement throughout the evolution of this project. Extra special thanks to Andrew O'Hehir of *Salon* (where Part One of this book was originally serialized in August and September of 2020) and Dale Peck of *The Evergreen Review* (where Parts Two and Three were published—in somewhat different form—in November of 2020 and June of 2021).

Notes

1 Barbara Fister, "The Librarian War Against QAnon," *The Atlantic*, Feb. 18, 2021 (accessed Sep. 24, 2021). Available at: https://www.theatlantic.com/education/archive/2021/02/how-librarians-can-fight-qanon/618047/.

2 Adam Serwer, "Trump's Plans for a Coup Are Now Public," *The Atlantic*, Sep. 23, 2021 (accessed Sep. 26, 2021). Available at: https://www.theatlantic.com/ideas/archive/2021/09/five-ways-donald-trump-tried-coup/620157/.

3 Kaleigh Rogers, "Trump Said QAnon 'Fights' Pedophilia. But the Group Has Made It Harder To Protect Kids," FiveThirtyEight, Oct. 15, 2020 (accessed Sep. 26, 2021). Available at: https://fivethirtyeight.com/features/qanons-obsession-with-savethechildren-is-making-it-harder-to-save-kids-from-traffickers/.

4 Marshall McLuhan, *The Gutenberg Galaxy* (New York: Signet, 1969 [1962]), p. 259.

5 Hunter S. Thompson, *Fear and Loathing in Las Vegas* (New York: Vintage, 1998 [1971]), p. 131.

6 Terry Gilliam, "Audio Commentary," *Fear and Loathing in Las Vegas* (DVD, The Criterion Collection, 2003).

7 Emily Writes, "Down the Rabbit Hole With the COVID-19 Conspiracy Theorists," Thespinoff.co.nz, March 17, 2020 (accessed July 5, 2020). Available at: https://thespinoff.co.nz/society/17-03-2020/emily-writes-down-the-rabbit-hole-with-the-covid-19-conspiracy-theorists/.

8 Mike Rothschild, "QAnon Is Attacking a Random Woman in a Disturbing and Dangerous Way," *Daily Dot*, March 22, 2019 (accessed July 5, 2020). Available at: https://www.dailydot.com/debug/qanon-rachel-chandler/.

9 Writes, "Down the Rabbit Hole With the COVID-19 Conspiracy Theorists."

10 Cory Doctorow, "Understanding Qanon," *Pluralistic* (blog), May 15, 2020 (accessed July 5, 2020). Available at: https://pluralistic.net/2020/05/15/out-here-everything-hurts/#q.

11 "Trump Approval Rating At Near Record Low, Quinnipiac University National Poll Finds," *Quinnipiac University Poll*, November 14, 2017 (accessed July 5, 2020). Available at: https://poll.qu.edu/Poll-Release-Legacy?releaseid=2500.

12   "1 of 2—Best of 'Underground Base Details! Part 8'—Gene De-
     code—B2T Show," YouTube.com (accessed July 5, 2020). Available
     at: https://www.youtube.com/watch?v=MY8Nfzcn1qQ. Since
     the writing of this book, the account that posted this and subse-
     quently-cited *B2T Show* YouTube videos has been deleted.

13   A.G. Pitts, "Devil Worship in Freemasonry," *The American Tyler* Vol.
     XVII, No. 24, June 15, 1903, p. 563.

14   "The Confession of Léo Taxil," *Grand Lodge of British Columbia
     and Yukon* (blog), April 2, 2001 (accessed July 5, 2020). Available at:
     https://freemasonry.bcy.ca/texts/taxil_confessed.html.

15   Leah Nelson, "Pastor Apologizes for Hate-filled Halloween
     Hand-out," *Southern Poverty Law Center*, November 2, 2011
     (accessed July 5, 2020). Available at: https://www.splcenter.org/
     hatewatch/2011/11/02/pastor-apologizes-hate-filled-hallow-
     een-hand-out.

16   Walter Kafton-Minkel, *Subterranean Worlds: 100,000 Years of
     Dragons, Dwarfs, the Dead, Lost Races & UFOs from Inside the Earth*
     (Port Townsend: Loompanics Unlimited, 1989), p. 141.

17   Fred Nadis, *The Man from Mars: Ray Palmer's Amazing Pulp Journey*
     (New York: Jeremy P. Tarcher/Penguin, 2013), pp. 67-68.

18   Mike Rothschild, "Inside the First Church of QAnon, Where
     Jesus Helps Fight the Deep State," *Daily Dot*, May 29, 2020
     (accessed July 5, 2020). Available at: https://www.dailydot.com/
     debug/qanon-church-omega-kingdom-ministries/.

19   Q, "4348," Qposts.online (accessed July 9, 2020). Available at:
     https://qposts.online/page/5.

20   Michael Barkun, "Failed Prophecies Won't Stop Trump's True
     Believers," *Foreign Policy*, November 8, 2018 (accessed July 5,
     2020). Available at: https://foreignpolicy.com/2018/11/08/failed-
     prophecies-wont-stop-trumps-true-believers/.

21   Timothy Burke, "How America's Largest Local TV Owner Turned
     Its News Anchors Into Soldiers In Trump's War On The Media,"
     Deadspin, March 31, 2018 (accessed July 5, 2020). Available at:
     https://deadspin.com/how-americas-largest-local-tv-owner-turned-
     its-news-anc-1824233490.

22   Brian Stelter, "Sinclair's New Media-bashing Promos Rankle
     Local Anchors," *CNN Business*, March 7, 2018 (accessed July 5,
     2020). Available at: https://money.cnn.com/2018/03/07/media/
     sinclair-broadcasting-promos-media-bashing/index.html.

23 Sarah Collins, "Kids in Cages and the Regulations that Protect Them," *Denver Law Review* (blog), November 11, 2019 (accessed July 6, 2020). Available at: https://fix8media-denverlaw.squarespace.com/dlr-online-article/kids-in-cages-and-the-regulations-that-protect-them.

24 Michael A. Aquino and Paul E. Vallely, "From PSYOP to MindWar: The Psychology of Victory," *Flow of Wisdom* (blog), July 7, 2013 (accessed July 5, 2020). Available at: https://flowofwisdom.files.wordpress.com/2013/07/mindwar-mindwar_co_authored_by_michael-aquino.pdf.

25 Robert Guffey, *Cryptoscatology: Conspiracy Theory As Art Form* (Walterville, OR: TrineDay, 2012), p. 34.

26 Alex Constantine, *Blood, Carnage and the Agent Provocateur* (Los Angeles: The Constantine Report, 1993), pp. 13-19.

27 *Out of Shadows*, YouTube.com (accessed July 5, 2020). Available at: https://www.youtube.com/watch?v=MY8Nfzcn1qQ. Since the writing of this book, the YouTube account that posted *Out of Shadows* has been deleted.

28 Ibid.

29 "The Hillary Clinton Cloning Program Does Exist!!," *Our New Earth News* (blog), April 12, 2019 (accessed July 5, 2020). Available at: https://www.ournewearthnews.com/2019/04/12/the-hillary-clinton-cloning-program-does-exist/.

30 "Dr. Peter Beter Audio Letter 46: Rockefeller; Cosmosphere; Modern Alliance – May 28, 1979," YouTube.com (accessed July 5, 2020). Available at: https://www.youtube.com/watch?v=3H1yX-pvVaKw&list=PLdtfE1_vu8Q66FrFpgGl0lHqsEYTJ1owt&index=46.

31 Police Against the New World Order, *Operation Vampire Killer 2000* (Phoenix, AZ: Police Against the New World Order, 1992), p. 1.

32 Ibid. p. 34.

33 "The Past American Century – The Cult Like Aspects of QAnon and Conspiracy Theories That Lead To Nowhere," *Porkins Policy Review* (blog), (accessed July 7, 2020). Available at: https://porkinspolicyreview.com/2019/05/28/the-past-american-century-the-cult-like-aspects-of-qanon-and-conspiracy-theories-that-lead-to-nowhere/.

34 Adam Goldman, "The Comet Ping Pong Gunman Answers Our Reporter's Questions," *The New York Times*, December 7, 2016 (accessed July 5, 2020). Available at: https://www.nytimes.com/2016/12/07/us/edgar-welch-comet-pizza-fake-news.html.

35   Stephanie K. Baer, "An Armed Man Spouting a Bizarre Right-Wing Conspiracy Theory Was Arrested After a Standoff at the Hoover Dam," *Buzzfeed News*, June 17, 2018 (accessed July 5, 2020). Available at: https://www.buzzfeednews.com/article/skbaer/qanon-believer-arrested-hoover-dam.

36   Andy Kroll, "John Podesta Is Ready to Talk About Pizzagate," *Rolling Stone*, December 9, 2018 (accessed July 5, 2020). Available at: https://www.rollingstone.com/politics/politics-features/john-podesta-pizzagate-766489/.

37   *Out of Shadows*, YouTube.com (accessed July 5, 2020). Available at: https://www.youtube.com/watch?v=MY8Nfzcn1qQ.

38   Ibid.

39   James Warren, "How a Bulldog TV Host Turned Lapdog in Trump Interview," *Poynter*, January 30, 2018 (accessed July 5, 2020). Available at: https://www.poynter.org/newsletters/2018/how-a-bulldog-tv-host-turned-lapdog-in-trump-interview/.

40   *Out of Shadows*.

41   "Professor Griff Discusses Occult Rituals in Hip Hop Part 2," YouTube.com (accessed July 5, 2020). Available at: https://www.youtube.com/watch?v=Iy4Ry8oKuoU.

42   Callie Ahlgrim, "Kanye West Said He'll Vote for Trump Because Buying Real Estate Is Better Now, and Former Fans Say It's 'Embarrassingly Hilarious'," *Insider*, April 16, 2020 (accessed July 5, 2020). Available at: https://www.insider.com/kanye-west-voting-trump-real-estate-interview-reactions-2020-4.

43   Mark Osborne, "Kanye West Announces He's Running for President," *ABC News*, July 4, 2020 (accessed July 7, 2020). Available at: https://abcnews.go.com/Entertainment/kanye-west-announced-running-president/story?id=71614805.

44   Alex Greenberger, "Microsoft Deletes Marina Abramovic Advertisement After Right-Wing Outcry Over Alleged Satanism," *ARTnews*, April 15, 2020 (accessed July 5, 2020). Available at: https://www.artnews.com/art-news/news/microsoft-deletes-marina-abramovic-campaign-satanism-1202683987/.

45   Nick Bryant, "Here Is Pedophile Billionaire Jeffrey Epstein's Little Black Book," *Gawker*, January 23, 2015 (accessed July 9, 2020). Available at: https://www.gawker.com/here-is-pedophile-billionaire-jeffrey-epsteins-little-b-1681383992.

46   Arthur Villasanta, "Jeffrey Epstein Death: Suicide Is 'Impossible,' Says Former Inmate," *International Business Times*, August 11,

2019 (accessed July 5, 2020). Available at: https://www.ibtimes.com/jeffrey-epstein-death-suicide-impossible-says-former-inmate-2812168.

47 "Cult Symbols – Gene Decode: Part 1. B2T Show," Apr. 30, 2020 (IS), YouTube.com (accessed July 5, 2020). Available at: https://www.youtube.com/watch?v=JJOXhFCty2s.

48 Daniel Bates, "Jeffrey Epstein Had Surveillance Cameras Hidden Throughout His Properties Worldwide in a 'Blackmail Scheme' to Extort His Powerful Friends, Victims Tell New Netflix Doc About the Pedophile," *Daily Mail*, May 27, 2020 (accessed July 5, 2020). Available at: https://www.dailymail.co.uk/news/article-8361607/Jeffrey-Epsteins-surveillance-cameras-blackmail-scheme-extort-powerful-friends.html.

49 "Americanuck Radio – 20191014," *Spreaker*, October 14, 2019 (accessed July 5, 2020). Available at: https://www.spreaker.com/user/icrn/americanuck-radio-20191014.

50 "Biography," *United States Army Pacific* (website), (accessed July 5, 2020). Available at: https://www.usarpac.army.mil/history2/dcg-Vallely.asp.

51 *Out of Shadows*, YouTube.com (accessed July 5, 2020). Available at: https://www.youtube.com/watch?v=MY8Nfzcn1qQ.

52 Michael A. Aquino and Paul E. Vallely, "From PSYOP to Mind-War: The Psychology of Victory," *Flow of Wisdom* (blog), July 7, 2013 (accessed July 5, 2020). Available at: https://flowofwisdom.files.wordpress.com/2013/07/mindwar-mindwar_co_authored_by_michael-aquino.pdf.

53 Ibid.

54 Greg Taylor, "Civil War Psy-Op: An Alternative Narrative of the QAnon Conspiracy Theory," *Daily Grail*, May 27, 2020 (accessed July 5, 2020). Available at: https://www.dailygrail.com/2020/05/civil-war-psy-op-an-alternative-narrative-of-the-qanon-conspiracy-theory/.

55 "Catfish," *Urban Dictionary* (accessed July 5, 2020). Available at: https://www.urbandictionary.com/define.php?term=catfish.

56 Marshall McLuhan and Barrington Nevitt, *Take Today: The Executive as Dropout* (New York: Harcourt Brace, 1972), p. 52. (The exact quote reads as follows: "All old technologies become 'art' forms.")

57 Hunter S. Thompson, *The Great Shark Hunt: Strange Tales from a Strange Time* (New York: Simon & Schuster, 2003 [1979]), p. 166.

58 Ibid. p. 162.

59   Ibid. p. 157.

60   Ibid. p. 160.

61   Ibid. p. 163.

62   Robert Anton Wilson, *Cosmic Trigger Volume I: Final Secret of the Illuminati* (Tempe, AZ: New Falcon, 1997 [1977]), p. 57.

63   Ibid. p. 59.

64   Jesse Walker, "Conspiracy Theory Is a Hoax Gone Right?," *New York magazine*, November 15, 2013 (accessed September 15, 2020). Available at: https://nymag.com/news/features/conspiracy-theories/operation-mindfuck/.

65   Robert Anton Wilson, *Cosmic Trigger Volume I: Final Secret of the Illuminati*, p. 63.

66   William S. Burroughs, *"The Revised Boy Scout Manual": An Electronic Revolution* (Columbus, OH: The Ohio State University Press, 2018), pp. 48-49.

67   Ibid. p. 48.

68   Ibid. p. 43.

69   Andrea Juno and V. Vale (eds.), *RE/Search #11: Pranks!* (San Francisco: RE/Search Publications, 1987), p. 63.

70   Ibid.

71   Ibid. pp. 59-64.

72   Marshall McLuhan and Barrington Nevitt, *Take Today: The Executive as Dropout* (New York: Harcourt Brace, 1972), pp. 5-6. (The exact quote reads as follows: *"Every process pushed far enough tends to reverse or flip suddenly."*)

73   Douglas Rushkoff, Interview, *In Other News*, Pacifica Radio, WBAI, New York, January 28, 2019. Available at: https://inothernewsradio.com/podcast/in-other-news-january-28-2019/.

74   Douglas Rushkoff, Lecture, "Douglas Rushkoff: Team Human," *Techonomy*, May 21, 2019 (accessed September 15, 2020). Available at: https://techonomy.com/video/team-human/.

75   Douglas Rushkoff, "Operation Mindfuck 2.0," *Medium*, April 24, 2020 (accessed September 15, 2020). Available at: https://medium.com/team-human/operation-mindfuck-2-0-358f9d237174.

76   David Neiwert, "What the Kek: Explaining the Alt-Right 'Deity' Behind Their 'Meme Magic,'" *Southern Poverty Law Center*, May 9, 2017 (accessed May 9, 2017). Available at: https://www.splcenter.org/hatewatch/2017/05/08/what-kek-explaining-alt-right-deity-behind-their-meme-magic.

77 "Americanuck Radio – 20191014," *Spreaker*, October 14, 2019 (accessed July 5, 2020). Available at: https://www.spreaker.com/user/icrn/americanuck-radio-20191014.

78 Daily News Editorial Board, "Playing with fire: Trump's let-it-burn cruelty for California," *New York Daily News*, August 22, 2020 (accessed September 17, 2020). Available at: https://www.nydailynews.com/opinion/99-reasons-to-dump-trump/ny-edit-99-wildfires-20200822-h5c42rwhgrgivmsmbwv2ad3yzq-story.html.

79 Billy Anania, "The Story Behind a Misunderstood Satanic Monument," *Hyperallergic*, September 16, 2020 (accessed September 17, 2020). Available at: https://hyperallergic.com/587195/.

80 Q, "4379," Qalerts.app (accessed September 17, 2020). Available at: https://qalerts.app/?n=4379.

81 Marc-André Argentino, "The Church of QAnon: Will Conspiracy Theories Form the Basis of a New Religious Movement?," *The Conversation*, May 18, 2020 (accessed September 17, 2020). Available at: https://theconversation.com/the-church-of-qanon-will-conspiracy-theories-form-the-basis-of-a-new-religious-movement-137859.

82 William Haupt III, "Is Capitalistic Socialism Next?," *The Center Square*, March 4, 2019 (accessed September 15, 2020). Available at: https://www.thecentersquare.com/national/op-ed-is-capitalistic-socialism-next/article_b989d884-3e77-11e9-8076-0f21174b7e22.html.

83 "Company Profile," The MASY Group (accessed September 18, 2020). Available at: http://www.masygroup.com/about/.

84 "About EKS Group, LLC," CorporateGray.com (accessed September 18, 2020). Available at: https://www.corporategray.com/employers/31641/public_profile.

85 Jeffrey Goldberg, "Trump: Americans Who Died in War Are 'Losers' and 'Suckers,'" *The Atlantic*, September 3, 2020 (accessed September 15, 2020). Available at: https://www.theatlantic.com/politics/archive/2020/09/trump-americans-who-died-at-war-are-losers-and-suckers/615997/.

86 Patrick Buchanan, "Pat Buchanan's Response to Norman Podhoretz's Op-Ed November 5, 1999 *Wall Street Journal*," *Internet Archive*, November 5, 1999 (accessed September 15, 2020). Available at: https://web.archive.org/web/20080511153332/http://www.buchanan.org/pma-99-1105-wallstjl.html.

87   "Trump Blamed 'Both Sides' for Charlottesville Attacks and
      People Aren't Happy," *The New Arab*, August 16, 2017 (accessed
      September 15, 2020). Available at: https://english.alaraby.co.uk/
      opinion/trump-blames-both-sides-charlottesville-twitter-reacts.

88   Kelly McLaughlin, "The Trump Campaign Has Knowingly Taken
      Thousands of Dollars from a neo-Nazi Leader and Other Racists,"
      Business Insider, August 31, 2020 (accessed September 17, 2020).
      Available at: https://www.businessinsider.com/trump-campaign-
      accepted-money-from-neo-nazi-leader-other-racists-2020-8.

89   "MUST HEAR FOR T.I.'s…," YouTube.com (accessed Septem-
      ber 15, 2020). Available at: https://www.youtube.com/watch?v=-
      0BLIXA2FAl0&feature=youtu.be.

90   Tracy Alloway and Lily Katz, "Private Prison Stocks Are Surg-
      ing After Trump's Win," *Bloomberg*, November 9, 2016 (accessed
      September 15, 2020). Available at: https://www.bloomberg.com/
      news/articles/2016-11-09/private-prison-stocks-are-surging-af-
      ter-trump-s-win.

91   Anna-Louise Jackson, Rita Nazareth and Eliza Ronalds-Hannan,
      "U.S. Stocks Rise, Treasuries Fall as Trump Win Spurs Growth
      Bets," *Bloomberg*, November 9, 2016 (accessed September 15,
      2020). Available at: https://www.bloomberg.com/news/arti-
      cles/2016-11-08/stocks-higher-with-mexican-peso-as-vote-
      count-nears-yen-weakens.

92   Joe Gould, "Trump Calls US Defense Spending 'Crazy,' Pledg-
      es Talks with Putin and Xi," *Defense News*, December 3, 2018
      (accessed August 6, 2019). Available at: https://www.defensenews.
      com/congress/budget/2018/12/03/trump-calls-us-defense-
      spending-crazy-pledging-talks-with-putin-and-xi/.

93   Sandra Erwin, "Trump's 2020 Budget Increases Defense Spending
      By 5 Percent, Funds Space Force," *Space News*, March 11, https://
      spacenews.com/trumps-2020-budget-increases-defense-spending-
      by-5-percent-funds-space-force/.

94   Walter Bowart, *Operation Mind Control* (Ft. Bragg: Flatland Edi-
      tions, 1994 [1978]), Chp. 41, pp. 3-19.

95   Emily Writes, "Down the Rabbit Hole With the COVID-19
      Conspiracy Theorists," *The Spinoff*, March 17, 2020 (accessed
      Nov. 13, 2020). Available at: https://thespinoff.co.nz/socie-
      ty/17-03-2020/emily-writes-down-the-rabbit-hole-with-the-
      covid-19-conspiracy-theorists.

96   "The Great Election Sting!," *Blessed 2 Teach* (blog), Nov. 4, 2020
     (accessed Nov. 7, 2020). Available at: https://blessed2teach.
     com/the-great-election-sting-amanda-gene-live-b2t-show-
     nov-4-2020-2/.

97   Maura Ewing, Rachel Weiner, Craig Timberg and Mark Ber-
     man, "Two Charged With Carrying Weapons Near Philadelphia
     Vote-counting Site Amid Election Tensions," *The Washington
     Post*, Nov. 6, 2020 (accessed Nov. 13, 2020). Available at: https://
     www.washingtonpost.com/nation/2020/11/06/philadelphia-at-
     tack-plot-vote-count-election/.

98   "Armed Men Arrested Outside Counting Centre in Philadel-
     phia Were Trying to Deliver Fake Ballots," *Times of India*, Nov. 7,
     2020 (accessed Nov. 13, 2020). Available at: https://timesofindia.
     indiatimes.com/world/us/us-presidential-elections/armed-men-
     arrested-outside-counting-centre-in-philadelphia-were-trying-to-
     deliver-fake-ballots-reports/articleshow/79098427.cms.

99   Will Sommer, "QAnon Promotes Pedo-Ring Conspiracy
     Theories. Now They're Stealing Kids," *Daily Beast*, Aug. 16,
     2020 (accessed Nov. 13, 2020). Available at: https://www.the-
     dailybeast.com/qanon-promotes-pedo-ring-conspiracy-theo-
     ries-now-theyre-stealing-kids.

100 Edgar Allan Poe, "The Masque of the Red Death," *Cryptoscatology*
     (blog), March 23, 2020 (accessed November 14, 2020). Available
     at: http://cryptoscatology.blogspot.com/2020/03/the-masque-of-
     red-death.html.

101 Julia Alexander, "YouTube won't ban QAnon content, but will
     remove videos that could promote violence," *The Verge*, Oct. 15,
     2020 (accessed Nov. 13, 2020). Available at: https://www.theverge.
     com/2020/10/15/21517640/youtube-qanon-content-policy-up-
     date-hate-harassment-ban-facebook-pinterest.

102 "The Great Election Sting! Part 3 – PA Rescinded!" *Blessed 2
     Teach* (blog), Nov. 9, 2020 (accessed Nov. 13, 2020). Available at:
     https://blessed2teach.com/the-great-election-sting-part-3-pa-re-
     scinded-b2t-show-nov-9-2020-is-2/.

103 Ibid.

104 Greg Palast, "Florida's Flawed 'Voter-cleansing' Program,"
     Greg Palast (blog), Dec. 4, 2000 (accessed Nov. 14, 2020). Available
     at: https://www.gregpalast.com/floridas-flawed-voter-cleans-
     ing-program-saloncoms-politics-story-of-the-year/.

105 Q, "4949," Qalerts.app/ (accessed Nov. 13, 2020). Available at: https://qalerts.app/?n=4949.

106 Q, "4951," Qalerts.app/ (accessed Nov. 13, 2020). Available at: https://qalerts.app/?n=4951.

107 "The Great Election Sting – Part 6. 1984 Censorship," *Blessed 2 Teach* (blog), Nov. 13, 2020 (accessed Nov. 15, 2020). Available at: https://blessed2teach.com/the-great-election-sting-part-6-1984-censorship-b2t-show-nov-13-2020-is-2/.

108 Q, "4944," Qalerts.app/ (accessed Nov. 13, 2020). Available at: https://qalerts.app/?n=4944.

109 Q, "4945," Qalerts.app/ (accessed Nov. 13, 2020). Available at: https://qalerts.app/?n=4945.

110 Q, "4946," Qalerts.app/ (accessed Nov. 13, 2020). Available at: https://qalerts.app/?n=4946.

111 "DominionGate! The Great Election Sting! Part 8. B2T Nov 15, 2020," *Blessed 2 Teach* (blog), Dec. 15, 2020 (accessed Dec. 18, 2020). Available at: https://blessed2teach.com/dominiongate-the-great-election-sting-part-8-b2t-nov-15-2020-is-2/.

112 "I Can't Keep It Up," Dec. 25, 2020 (accessed Jan. 12, 2021). Available at: https://searchvoat.co/v/announcements/4169936.

113 "Gene on the Election. The Great Election Sting! Part 11. B2T Nov 22, 2020," YouTube.com, Nov 22, 2020 (accessed Jan. 10, 2021). Available at: https://www.youtube.com/watch?v=IsWxl-AyzzE.

114 "Grant Morrison: Freaks Like Us," *Team Human*, Dec. 21, 2020 (accessed Jan. 13, 2021). Available at: https://www.teamhuman.fm/episodes/166-grant-morrison.

115 Sanjana Karanth, "Armed Michiganders Gather Outside Secretary of State's Home to Deny Voting Results," *HuffPost*, Dec. 6, 2020 (accessed Jan. 10, 2021). Available: https://www.huffpost.com/entry/armed-michigan-protest-secretary-of-state-home-election_n_5fcd9995c5b63a1534530e6d.

116 Chris Matthews, "Electoral College Confirms Joe Biden as President-Elect Amid Threats of Violence and Trump Protests," *MarketWatch*, Dec. 14, 2020 (accessed Jan. 10, 2021). Available at: https://www.marketwatch.com/story/electoral-college-meets-amid-threats-of-violence-and-trump-protests-11607961822.

117 Kenneth Garger, "Former Houston Cop Arrested for Attacking Repairman Over Bizarre Voter Fraud Claims," *New York Post*, Dec. 15, 2020 (accessed Jan. 10, 2021). Available at: https://nypost.

com/2020/12/15/former-houston-cop-charged-after-trying-to-prove-2020-election-fraud/.

118 "Game Over. The Great Election Sting! Part 29. B2T Show Dec. 20, 2020," *Blessed 2 Teach* (blog), Dec. 20, 2020 (accessed Jan. 10, 2021). Available at: https://blessed2teach.com/game-over-the-great-election-sting-part-29-b2t-show-dec-20-2020-is-2/.

119 "Four People Arrested in Unlawful Assembly Outside Oregon State Capitol; 1 Person Sought," KPTV.com, Dec. 21, 2020 (accessed Jan. 10, 2021). Available at: https://www.kptv.com/news/four-people-arrested-in-unlawful-assembly-outside-oregon-state-capitol-1-person-sought/article_e91ed20e-4418-11eb-916a-0772967ddbf4.html#:~:text=SALEM%2C%20OR%20(KPTV)%20%E2%80%93,according%20to%20Oregon%20State%20Police.&text=At%2010%3A30%20a.m.%2C%20a,Ryan%20Lyles%2C%2041%2C%20arrest.

120 "Gene Decode on Decoding! Part 2: Word from the Lord—Amanda Grace. B2T Show Dec 21, 2020," *Blessed 2 Teach* (blog), Dec. 21, 2020 (accessed Jan. 10, 2021). Available at: https://blessed2teach.com/gene-decode-on-decoding-part-2-word-from-the-lord-amanda-grace-b2t-show-dec-21-2020-is-2/.

121 Robert Anton Wilson, "Introduction: The Spaghetti Theory of Conspiracy" in *The Illuminati Conspiracy: The Sapiens System* by Donald Holmes, 2nd ed., (Tempe, AZ: New Falcon, 1993), pp. 17-18.

122 Ben Collins, "As Trump Meets With QAnon Influencers, the Conspiracy's Adherents Beg for Dictatorship," *NBC News*, Dec. 22, 2020 (accessed Jan. 10, 2021). Available at: https://www.nbcnews.com/tech/internet/trump-meets-qanon-influencers-conspiracy-theorys-adherents-beg-dictatorship-n1252144.

123 Laura Wamsley, "Shock and Dismay After Trump Pardons Blackwater Guards Who Killed 14 Iraqi Civilians," *NPR*, Dec. 23, 2020 (accessed Jan. 10, 2021). Available at: https://www.npr.org/2020/12/23/949679837/shock-and-dismay-after-trump-pardons-blackwater-guards-who-killed-14-iraqi-civil.

124 Jacob Heilbrunn, "The Neocons vs. Donald Trump," *The New York Times*, Mar. 10, 2016 (accessed Jan. 24, 2021). Available at: https://www.nytimes.com/2016/03/13/opinion/sunday/the-neocons-vs-donald-trump.html?searchResultPosition=1.

125 John Bowden, "UN Says Trump Blackwater Pardons Violate International Law," *The Hill*, Dec. 30, 2020 (accessed Jan. 10,

2021). Available at: https://thehill.com/homenews/administration/532065-un-says-trump-blackwater-pardons-violate-international-law/.

126 Adi Robertson, "AT&T Recovers from Multi-state Outage After Nashville Bombing," *The Verge*, Dec. 28, 2020 (accessed Jan. 10, 2021). Available at: https://www.theverge.com/2020/12/28/22202822/att-outage-nashville-christmas-bombing.

127 Ben Ashford, "Nashville Bomber Anthony Warner 'Targeted AT&T After His Father Who Worked for Subsidiary Died of Dementia—Fueling His Conspiracy Theory That 5G Is Killing People,'" *Daily Mail*, Dec. 27, 2020 (accessed Jan. 10, 2021). Available at: https://www.dailymail.co.uk/news/article-9091781/Death-Nashville-Christmas-bombers-father-fueled-5G-conspiracy-theory.html.

128 "Gene Decode's Insights on Jan 6. B2T Show Jan 2, 2021," YouTube.com, Jan. 2, 2021 (accessed Jan. 10, 2021). Available at: https://www.youtube.com/watch?v=XGDLrXwP5pQ&feature=emb_logo.

129 Amy Gardner, "'I Just Want to Find 11,780 Votes': In extraordinary hour-long call, Trump pressures Georgia secretary of state to recalculate the vote in his favor," *The Washington Post*, Jan. 3, 2021 (accessed Jan. 10, 2021). Available at: https://www.washingtonpost.com/politics/trump-raffensperger-call-georgia-vote/2021/01/03/d45acb92-4dc4-11eb-bda4-615aaefd0555_story.html.

130 Amy Gardner and Paulina Frozi, "Here's the full transcript and audio of the call between Trump and Raffensperger," *The Washington Post*, Jan. 5, 2021 (accessed Jan. 10, 2021). Available at: https://www.washingtonpost.com/politics/trump-raffensperger-call-transcript-georgia-vote/2021/01/03/2768e0cc-4ddd-11eb-83e3-322644d82356_story.html.

131 "All 10 living former defense secretaries: Involving the military in election disputes would cross into dangerous territory," *The Washington Post*, Jan. 3, 2021 (accessed Jan. 10, 2021). Available at: https://www.washingtonpost.com/opinions/10-former-defense-secretaries-military-peaceful-transfer-of-power/2021/01/03/2a23d52e-4c4d-11eb-a9f4-0e668b9772ba_story.html.

132 Jaclyn Diaz, "In Op-Ed, 10 Ex-Defense Secretaries Say Military Has No Role in Election Dispute," *NPR*, Jan. 4, 2021

(accessed Jan. 10, 2021). Available at: https://www.npr.
org/2021/01/04/953119935/in-op-ed-10-ex-defense-secretaries-
say-military-has-no-role-in-election-dispute.

133 Ted Barrett, Peter Nickeas, and Manu Raju, "US Capitol Secured,
4 Dead After Rioters Stormed the Halls of Congress to Block
Biden's Win," *CNN*, Jan. 7, 2021 (accessed Jan. 10, 2021). Available
at: https://www.cnn.com/2021/01/06/politics/us-capitol-lock-
down/index.html.

134 David Covucci, "Major QAnon Figure Stands Atop House Chamber in Fur Costume," *Daily Dot*, Jan. 6, 2021 (accessed Jan. 10,
2021). Available at: https://www.dailydot.com/debug/qanon-sha-
man-house-chamber-jake-angeli/.

135 "Cabal Chooses Treason. Pick Your Side. B2T Show Jan 7, 2021,"
Blessed 2 Teach (blog), Jan. 7, 2021 (accessed Jan. 10, 2021). Available
at: https://blessed2teach.com/cabal-chooses-treason-pick-your-
side-b2t-show-jan-7-2021-is-2/.

136 Brandy Zadrozny and Mosheh Gains, "Woman killed in Capitol was Trump supporter who embraced conspiracy theories,"
NBC News, Jan. 7, 2021 (accessed Jan. 10, 2021). Available at:
https://www.nbcnews.com/news/us-news/woman-killed-cap-
itol-was-trump-supporter-who-embraced-conspiracy-theo-
ries-n1253285.

137 "Rick Rene (B2T)," LinkedIn.com (accessed Jan. 10, 2021). Available at: https://www.linkedin.com/in/rickrene.

138 Ronan Farrow, "An Air Force Combat Veteran Breached the Senate," *The New Yorker*, Jan. 9, 2021 (accessed Jan. 12, 2021). Available
at: https://www.newyorker.com/news/news-desk/an-air-force-
combat-veteran-breached-the-senate.

139 Nick Visser, "FBI Arrests 2 Men Seen With Zip Tie Restraints
During U.S. Capitol Riot," *HuffPost*, Jan. 10, 2021 (accessed Jan.
12, 2021). Available at: https://www.huffpost.com/entry/fbi-ar-
rests-zip-tie-capitol-rioters_n_5ffb8e6fc5b63642b6fce5dd.

140 Claire Lampen, "Terrifying Details About the Capitol Hill Riots
Keep Coming Out," *The Cut*, Jan. 10, 2021 (accessed Jan. 12,
2021). Available at: https://www.thecut.com/2021/01/capitol-ri-
ots-lawmakers-and-journalists-chilling-accounts.html.

141 Mary Papenfuss, "Roger Stone Calls for Trump to 'Declare Martial
Law' to Seize Power If He Loses," *HuffPost*, Sep. 12, 2021 (accessed
Jan. 11, 2021). Available at: https://www.huffpost.com/entry/

roger-stone-martial-law-donald-trump-election_n_5f5d3e28c5b-62874bc1dd6d2.

142 Ibid.

143 Dan Koiss, "They Were Out for Blood," *Slate*, Jan. 8, 2021 (accessed Jan. 12, 2021). Available at: https://slate.com/news-and-politics/2021/01/was-there-a-plan-for-hostages-or-killings-at-the-capitol.html.

144 Jacques Ellul, *Propaganda: The Formation of Men's Attitudes* (New York: Vintage, 1973 [1965]), pp.151-152.

145 Kyle Cheney and Sarah Ferris, "Dems Demand Details of 'Suspicious' Capitol Visitors Day Before Attack," *Politico*, Jan. 12, 2021 (accessed Jan. 21, 2021). Available at: https://www.politico.com/news/2021/01/12/mikie-sherrill-capitol-hill-attack-458655.

146 Kyle Mantyla, "Conspiracy Theorist Cirsten Weldon Claims Trump Has Been Targeted for Assassination 'Over 50' Times and Will Be Targeted Again in July," *Right Wing Watch*, June 22, 2020 (accessed Mar. 7, 2021). Available at: https://www.rightwingwatch.org/post/conspiracy-theorist-cirsten-weldon-claims-trump-has-been-targeted-for-assassination-over-50-times-and-will-be-targeted-again-in-july/.

147 "Gene Decode #30 DUMBS and Trumps Nesara," Jan. 16, 2021 (accessed Mar. 7, 2021). Available at: https://www.youtube.com/watch?v=8UWVdLPgiZA.

148 "Hold the Line!. Gene DUMBs Update. B2T Show Jan 20, 2021," *Blessed 2 Teach* (blog), Jan. 20, 2021 (accessed Jan. 21, 2021). Available at: https://www.youtube.com/watch?v=gAj4Ktu1mCs.

149 "Gene Decode! Africa Underground Bases: Mpumalanga, Limpopo. B2T Show Mar 4, 2021," *Blessed 2 Teach* (blog), Mar. 4, 2021 (accessed Mar. 4, 2021). Available at: https://blessed2teach.com/gene-decode-africa-underground-bases-mpumalanga-limpopo-b2t-show-mar-4-2021-is-2/.

150 Katelyn Polantz, "Sidney Powell Argues in New Court Filing That No Reasonable People Would Believe Her Election Fraud Claims," *CNN*, March 23, 2021 (accessed March 29, 2021). Available at: https://www.cnn.com/2021/03/22/politics/sidney-powell-dominion-lawsuit-election-fraud/index.html.

151 "Take Our Country Back! 2nd Amendment Attack. B2T Show, Wed Mar 24, 2021," *iHeart*, Mar. 24, 2021 (accessed Mar. 30, 2021). Available at: https://www.iheart.com/

podcast/269-blessed2teach-77149916/episode/take-our-country-back-2nd-amendment-80145503/#.

152 Cheryl Teh, "An HBO filmmaker may have uncovered the identity of 'Q,' the shady figure behind QAnon," *Business Insider*, Apr. 5, 2021 (accessed May 2, 2021). Available at: https://www.businessinsider.com/hbo-filmmaker-may-have-uncovered-potential-identity-of-q-qanon-2021-4.

153 Eric Hananoki, "Trump touted the endorsement of an nnhinged QAnon conspiracy theorist and birther," *Media Matters*, Oct. 6, 2020 (accessed May 2, 2021). Available at: https://www.mediamatters.org/qanon-conspiracy-theory/trump-touted-endorsement-paul-e-vallely-unhinged-qanon-conspiracy-theorist.

154 Olivia Messer, "Mesa College Fires Professor Who Promoted QAnon Conspiracy Theory," *Daily Beast*, Sep. 17, 2019 (accessed May 2, 2021). Available at: https://www.thedailybeast.com/mesa-college-fires-professor-who-promoted-qanon-conspiracy-theory.

155 James Crowley, "Viral Video Shows Teacher Claiming Antifa, Not Trump Supporters, Stormed the Capitol," *Newsweek*, Jan. 14, 2021 (accessed May 2, 2021). Available at: https://www.newsweek.com/teacher-antifa-trump-supporters-viral-video-stormed-capitol-1561699.

156 Nina Agrawal, "Chapman University will not fire law professor who spoke at pro-Trump Capitol rally," *Los Angeles Times*, Jan. 13, 2021 (accessed May 2, 2021). Available at: https://www.latimes.com/california/story/2021-01-13/chapman-university-will-not-fire-john-eastman.

157 Joshua Zitser and Sophia Ankel, "A Trump-loving insurrectionist and a convicted stalker are among 36 QAnon supporters running for Congress in 2022," *Business Insider*, June 27, 2021 (accessed Sept. 9, 2021). Available at: https://www.businessinsider.com/the-36-qanon-supporters-running-congress-in-the-2022-midterms-2021-6.

158 Will Sommer, "Maxine Waters Foe Omar Navarro Gets Out of Jail And Attempts to Destroy Fellow Republican," *Daily Beast*, July 9, 2020 (accessed Sept. 10, 2021). Available at: https://www.thedailybeast.com/california-rep-maxine-waters-foe-omar-navarro-gets-out-of-jail-and-attempts-to-destroy-fellow-republican.

159 Storm Gifford, "Failed Politician and QAnon Backer DeAnna Lorraine Roasted After Writing That George Floyd's Family

Was Offered 'Free Meth' to Speak at Convention," *New York Daily News*, Aug. 18, 2020 (accessed Sept. 10, 2021). Available at: https://www.nydailynews.com/news/national/ny-qanon-sup-porter-free-meth-20200819-yrqyewitkrd7pnniyc7psigfsa-story. html.

160 Zitser and Ankel, "A Trump-loving insurrectionist and a convict-ed stalker are among 36 QAnon supporters running for Congress in 2022."

161 Mia Jankowicz ,"Mike Lindell set August 13 as the date in his bonkers theory that Trump will be reinstated as president," *Business Insider*, July 6, 2021 (accessed Sept. 8, 2021). Available at: https://www.businessinsider.com/mike-lindell-claims-august-13-trump-reinstatement-2021-7.

162 Khaleda Rahman, "MyPillow Products Will No Longer Be Sold by These Companies," *Newsweek*, Jan. 9, 2021 (accessed Sept. 8, 2021). Available at: https://www.newsweek.com/mypillow-products-no-longer-stocked-these-companies-1562510.

163 Jean Yamamura, "Matthew Coleman Influenced by 'QAnon and Illuminati Conspiracy Theories' to Kill His Children, Affidavit Says," *Santa Barbara Independent*, Aug. 11, 2021 (accessed Sept. 8, 2021). Available at: https://www.independent.com/2021/08/11/matthew-coleman-was-influenced-by-qanon-and-illuminati-con-spiracy-theories-to-kill-his-children-affidavit-says/.

164 Jamie Ross and Justin Rohrlich, "Surf School Owner Killed Kids After Being 'Enlightened' by QAnon," *Daily Beast*, Aug. 11, 2021 (accessed Sept. 8, 2021). Available at: https://www.thedailybeast.com/matthew-taylor-coleman-surf-school-owner-arrested-after-his-kids-1-and-3-found-stabbed-to-death.

165 Jenni Fink, "Trump 'Reinstatement Day' Latest Failure in Pre-dictions He'll Resume Presidency, Oust Biden," *Newsweek*, Aug. 13, 2021 (accessed Sept. 8, 2021). Available at: https://www.newsweek.com/trump-reinstatement-day-latest-failure-predic-tions-hell-resume-presidency-oust-biden-1619152.

166 "Kabul Chaos. Fauci Exposed. B2T Show, Aug 16, 2021", *Blessed 2 Teach* (blog), Aug. 16, 2021 (accessed Sept. 9, 2021). Available at: https://blessed2teach.com/kabul-chaos-fauci-exposed-b2t-show-aug-16-2021-is-2/.

167 "Jacob Chansley, Self-Styled 'QAnon Shaman,' Pleads Guilty To Felony Over Capitol Riot," *NPR*, Sept. 3, 2021

(accessed Sept. 8, 2021). Available at: https://www.npr.
org/2021/09/03/1034076581/an-arizona-man-who-wore-horns-
in-the-jan-6-capitol-riot-pleads-guilty-to-felony.

168 Drew Harwell and Craig Timberg, "'My faith is shaken': The
QAnon conspiracy theory faces a post-Trump identity crisis," *The
Washington Post*, Nov. 11, 2020 (accessed Nov. 13, 2020). Available
at: https://www.washingtonpost.com/technology/2020/11/10/
qanon-identity-crisis/.

169 Natalie Colarossi, "ACLU Counsel Warns of 'Unchecked Power'
of Twitter, Facebook After Trump Suspension," *Newsweek*, Jan. 9,
2021 (accessed Jan. 11, 2021). Available at: https://www.news-
week.com/aclu-counsel-warns-unchecked-power-twitter-face-
book-after-trump-suspension-1560248.

170 Ibid.

About the Author

Robert Guffey is a lecturer in the Department of English at California State University – Long Beach. His most recent books are *Widow of the Amputation and Other Weird Crimes* (Eraserhead Press, 2021) and *Bela Lugosi's Dead* (Crossroad Press, 2021). Guffey's previous books include the darkly satirical, apocalyptic novel *Until the Last Dog Dies* (Night Shade/ Skyhorse, 2017), the journalistic memoir *Chameleo: A Strange but True Story of Invisible Spies, Heroin Addiction, and Homeland Security* (OR Books, 2015), which *Flavorwire* called, "By many miles, the weirdest and funniest book of [the year]," the novella collection *Spies & Saucers* (PS Publishing, 2014), and *Cryptoscatology: Conspiracy Theory as Art Form* (2012). A graduate of the famed Clarion Writers Workshop in Seattle, he has written for numerous publications, among them *The Believer, Black Cat Mystery Magazine, The Evergreen Review, The Los Angeles Review of Books, The Mailer Review, Phantom Drift, Postscripts, Rosebud, Salon, The Third Alternative,* and *TOR.com.*